ALL ABOUT COMMODITIES

FROM THE INSIDE OUT

& Russell R. Wasendorf
Thomas A. McCafferty

PR...NY

ISBN 1-55738-459-2

Printed in the United States of America

IPC

2   3   4   5   6   7   8   9   0

To Cynthia, Monica and Colleen McCafferty and Russell R. Wasendorf, Jr.

And, many thanks to Geraldine Martinson for all her work on this book.

Contents

Preface

You could build a library with the short stories, novels, philosophical tomes—even movies, songs and operas—written about man's struggle with the future. "What will happen tomorrow?" is on our minds daily. Many people have become obsessed with it. A few have been reported, at least in the theater, to have sold their souls to uncover its secrets.

In our opinion, nothing written to date matches the drama that unfolds in the futures trading pits of Chicago and New York. Here the world's largest commodity futures markets explode each morning with the regularity of Old Faithful.

The last decade has seen this excitement spread over the globe. Trading volume records have been set in London, Paris, Sydney, and Tokyo. Even the spark of a commodity exchange has been struck in Moscow.

The international enthusiasm has not gone unnoticed in the United States. The two major Chicago exchanges launched GLOBEX, an electronic worldwide 24-hour trading "pit."

You share in all this excitement and opportunity when you learn to trade commodities. Additionally, since the futures markets are negatively correlated with stocks (one tends to gain while the other loses, and vice versa), you may even add some stability to your overall investment portfolio.

This book covers only the physical commodity markets (grains, livestock, precious and industrial metals, foods, fibers, petroleum, lumber and such) which are traded on regulated futures exchanges throughout the world. The financial futures markets (currencies, interest rates, stock market indexes, Treasury bills and bonds, and similar futures contracts) are not discussed, but the basic skills and knowledge you acquire trading the physical markets apply equally to the financial markets.

Lastly, we wish you luck. At the same time, we want to warn you that commodity trading is a very speculative investment not suited for everyone. It takes hard work to be successful. But the rewards can be so outstanding, we believe learning to trade them is worth the effort.

1

Rules of the Game—
How You Win or Lose

Key Concepts

◆ The basic concept of commodity trading is offsetting positions at more favorable prices than they were put on.

◆ Learning how to calculate profits or losses.

◆ Reading price quotations.

◆ Physical commodity contract specifications.

The basic concept underlying the commodity or futures markets is extremely simple. All you need to do is offset your position in the market with an equal but opposite position at a more favorable price.

For example, let's say you trade corn. You purchased one futures contract on the Chicago Board of Trade (CBOT) at $2.30. The contract calls for you to deliver the 5,000 bushels of Number 2 corn on a specific day in July. This means you are

---

1

"long" corn. It "be-longs" to you. Theoretically, you own 5,000 bushels of corn, just as surely as if you had a grain bin behind your home filled with kernels of corn.

Notice we use the word "theoretically." Most traders, approximately 97 percent, never deliver the commodity they "own." What they do is "sell" or offset their long position with a short position. That is an equal number of contracts, for the same delivery month (date) and on the same exchange. To offset your long corn position or contract, you would sell one corn contract on the Chicago Board of Trade. You agree to accept delivery of the 5,000 bushels of Number 2 corn on the specified date in July.

The delivery month just mentioned is an important concept. Corn is delivered in December, March, May, July, and September. If you bought corn to be delivered in July, you must sell corn to be taken delivery of in July to offset your position.

If you are long five September CBOT corn contracts at $2.30, and you wanted to offset your position, what do you do? You sell five September CBOT corn contracts. If you bought corn on the CBOT or the Kansas City exchange, you must offset on that exchange.

To correctly offset a position, all the specifications must be the same. This means commodity, number of contracts, exchange, and delivery month. One contract negates the other.

All the other specifications of the contract are standardized. For example, the CBOT corn contract calls for 5,000 bushels (quantity), of Number 2 Yellow corn (quality and type) at an elevator approved by the exchange (location), on a specific delivery date. In its simplest form, you make money in futures trading by doing one of the following:

Buy Low-Sell High

Buy High-Sell Higher

Sell High-Buy Low

Sell Low-Buy Lower

Price is a very relative relationship in commodity trading. Nobody ever knows how high or how low a contract can go.

Here are some examples of how to calculate the results of trades.

Grains: Long Soybean Trade

Initial Position: Buy one March Soybean CBOT contract at $6.00/bu.

Offsetting Position: Sell one March Soybean CBOT contract at $6.50/bu.

Net gain or (loss): $0.50/bu.

Profit (Loss) per contract: $2,500.00

In this example, we bought 5,000 bushels of soybeans at $6.00 per bushel and sold them at $6.50 per bushel for a $0.50 profit per bushel or $2,500.00 (5,000/bu. X $0.50). We traded on the Chicago Board of Trade. If we had done the same trade on the MidAmerica Commodity Exchange, we would have made $500.00 because MidAm contracts call for 1,000-bushel contracts, instead of 5,000 bushels.

Meats: Short Live Cattle Trade

Initial Position: Sell one August Live Cattle CME contract at $0.85/lb.

Offsetting Position: Buy one August Live Cattle CME contract at $0.65/lb.

Net gain or (loss): $0.20/lb.

Profit (loss) per contract: $8,000.00

Here we sold high and bought back at a lower price for a profit of $0.20 per pound. This amounts to $8,000.00, since the Chicago Mercantile Exchange (CME) live cattle contract calls for 40,000 pounds of beef (40,000 lbs. X $0.20).

Metals: Long Silver Trade

Initial Position: Buy one September COMEX silver contract at $5.00/oz.

Offsetting Position: Sell one September COMEX silver contract at $4.50/oz.

Net gain or (loss): ($0.50/oz.)

Profit (Loss) per contract: ($2,500.00)

On this trade, we lost $2,500.00. We bought high and sold low, the opposite of what we expected would happen. The Commodity Exchange, Inc. (COMEX) contract contains 5,000 troy ounces of not less than .999 fine silver.

Food/Fiber: Short Sugar Trade

Initial Position: Sell one January sugar CSCE contract at $0.12/lb.

Offsetting Position: Buy one January sugar CSCE contract at $0.10/lb.

Net gain or (loss) per unit: $0.02/lb.

Profit (Loss) per contract: $2,240.00

Our sugar trade netted $0.02 per pound. The Coffee, Sugar, Cocoa Exchange (CSCE) sugar contract is composed of 50 long tons or 112,000 pounds of raw cane sugar.

Petroleum: Long Crude Oil

Initial Position: Buy one December Crude Oil NYME contract at $20.50

Offsetting Position: Sell one December Crude Oil NYME contract at $20.55

Net gain or (loss) per unit: $0.05

Profit (Loss) per contract: $50.00

The New York Mercantile Exchange (NYME), contract contains 1,000 barrels. It is traded in dollars per barrel with $0.01 equaling $10.00. Therefore, a five-penny profit equals $50.00.

From these examples, you can see that if you are long or "own" a commodity, you want it to increase in value. If you are short the commodity, you anticipate it declining in value. Most importantly—if your analysis of the direction of the trend is incorrect, you will lose money on your trade(s).

The commodity market is a zero-based market. At the end of each day, the books are balanced. All positions are balanced. The traders on the wrong side of the market pay the traders on the correct side of the market. This is done through adjustments to the money (equity) each trader has on deposit with the firm through which he/she trades.

If a trader's position(s) has lost money, and he/she does not have a sufficient amount on deposit, a margin call is issued to the trader. This is an immediate demand for more equity. The brokerage firm may require the money be wired to them within hours, or a check sent via overnight courier within a day or two at the most. If the margin call is not honored, the brokerage firm may close out the trader's position. It may also take various other steps, some legal, to recover any amount due, if the receipts from closing out the position(s) are not sufficient to cover the loss.

Closing out a trader's position to pay a margin call can be expensive from another standpoint. The market being traded may be making a short term retracement against the trader's position. Shortly afterwards, it could continue to go the way the trader anticipates-generating profits. This gain would be lost if the trader failed to maintain sufficient equity or send additional money to meet a margin call.

Also keep in mind the profits and losses discussed so far are exclusive of what are known as transaction costs. These include your broker's commission, plus fees charged by the exchanges, industry, government regulators, and the firm that executes the trade (called the clearing firm). All these costs amount to anywhere from $30.00-$40.00 on the low end to $100.00-$125.00 on the high side. In the crude oil example, the $50.00 profit may not have been enough to cover the transaction costs.

Key Concept Summary

You must know the following information about any commodity (futures contract) you are trading in order to place the initial order, offset that position, and calculate your profit or loss:

A. Quantity—Number of contracts being traded.

B. Contract Month—The month the commodity is to be delivered to traders holding short positions and by traders holding long positions. This is the month the contract expires. In just about every case, investors offset before the expiration date.
There may be contracts for the same month spread over more than one year. In these cases, you need to know and specify the year when placing orders.

C. Contract Size—The size of the contract being traded can vary by exchange.

D. Exchange—Be sure to offset a position on the same exchange where you initiated the original position. If you don't, you'll be opening a completely new position.

E. Fill—This is the price you get when your orders are actually bought and/or sold in the pits of the exchanges. You need to know your fill prices to calculate your profits or losses.

F. Fees—Your account will be debited the broker's commissions, plus exchange, clearing and regulatory fees each time a trade is offset. With commodity futures, fees are traditionally charged when positions are closed (offset), but not always. Some clearing firms charge half the commissions the day the orders are filled. For options on commodities, it is common for all the transaction costs to be charged when the initial order is filled.

Dollar Value of Ticks

This discussion of profits and losses brings up the subject of ticks and their value. Ticks are a shortcut method brokers use to quickly calculate the changes in the value of commodity futures contracts. You'll hear your broker say things like: "Corn was up two ticks today, just as we expected."

A tick, or more correctly a minimum tick, is the smallest increment of change permitted in the price of a commodity. This terminology is a throwback to the days when ticker tapes were used to communicate prices. On today's modern quotation equipment, mainly computers, it is the minimum price movement displayed on the screen (CRT), just as it was the minimum change sent over the ticker tape.

The grains, for example, have minimum ticks of one-fourth of one cent. This calculates to $12.50 on CBOT contracts ($0.0025 X 5,000 bushels). Therefore, the two-tick move referred to earlier is a $25.00 per contract move.

Keep in mind that different exchanges may have different contract and tick sizes for the same commodity. The Mid American Exchange (MidAm) has a 1,000 bushel corn contract and a one-eighth of a cent tick for corn. One MidAm tick would only be $1.25, or $2.50 for the two-tick move for corn mentioned earlier.

As you can see from these two examples, a tick may be less than a full-cent move. Therefore, you may want to memorize the value of a $0.01 move for the commodities you trade regularly. On the major grain contracts, it's a simple calculation. You just divide 5,000 by 100, which means a $0.01 move equals $50.00. Knowing this value comes in handy when you get pricing information from your car radio or television. Don't forget on the MidAmerica Exchange, where they trade "mini" contracts, you would be dealing with 1,000 bushel contracts and $0.01 values of $10.00, rather than $50.00.

At the end of this chapter, you'll find a listing of all the vital information regarding contracts, delivery months, exchanges, tick prices, dollar values of $0.01, or $1.00 price moves. Refer to this table to obtain the information you need to answer the worksheet questions also at the end of this chapter.

Reading Price Quotations

Depending on how the markets are trading and the type of trading you do, you'll need to know how to check the prices of commodity futures contracts. Like stocks and other financial instruments, the various commodity contracts have abbreviations.

Also, you need to know the abbreviation of the delivery months. There can be a big difference in the price of a commodity between delivery months. With physical commodities, this is called the carrying cost—the cost for storage, insurance, interest and spoilage. For example, let's say it costs $0.04 per bushel per month to store corn at a grain elevator and insure it against fire and other accidents and acts of God. The difference in carrying costs between July corn and December corn would be $0.24 per bushel. Keep in mind that this figure of $0.04 varies regularly, depending on the demand for storage, interest rates and the cost of insurance. It also varies by commodity. For example, it costs more to store gold or silver in vaults than soybeans in a bin. But insuring grain is more costly than precious metals because more damaging things can happen to it.

Therefore, if you don't carefully check to see which delivery month the price quotation you are checking is for, you could be ecstatic or devastated depending on whether you are long or short. Below are the abbreviations for the delivery months. Abbreviations for the most common commodities are on page 9.

Abbreviations for Months

Month	Current Year	Following Year
JAN	F	D
FEB	G	E
MAR	H	I
APR	J	L
MAY	K	O
JUN	M	P

	Current	Following
Month	Year	Year
JUL	N	T
AUG	Q	R
SEP	U	B
OCT	V	C
NOV	X	W
DEC	Z	Y

There are two sets of abbreviations for each month because the futures contracts can roll from one year to the next. For example, June of the current year would be "M" and the June contract for the next year would be "P." At the end of the current year, the code for the following June changes from "P" to "M." You also need to double check with the quotation service you are using to make sure they use these conventions. But even if the letters vary, the theory will be the same.

A typical quotation page on a price quotation service might look like this:

LC	LC	FC	GC
M 7450	Q 7322	Q 8847	Q 3758
+27	+27	+25	−63

LH	LH	PB	SL
M 5705	N5535	N 5870	U 4595
+30	−7	−7	69

W	C	C	PL
N 2972	N 2450	Z 2472	N 3848
+12	−6	−14	+20

S	S	O	HG
N 5826	X 5942	N 1232	U 9750
−6	−2	+0	−50

SM	BO	CT	JO
Q 1770	N 2010	N 8720	N 11890
−1	+2	+39	+10

Note that we say "might" look like this. The above is typical, but there is no standard look. Quotation systems vary from one supplier to the next, but there is some general similarity. If you get a good feel for this presentation, you'll be able to figure out most.

The abbreviation for the commodity is above each price quotation. The top row reads: LC = Live Cattle; LC = Live Cattle; FC = Feeder Cattle; GC = Gold. The letter that is in the first place of the second line of each quotation designates the month. For example, row one includes: M = June; Q = August; Q = August; Q = August. The remainder of this line is the most current price. Line three is the change from the previous day's closing price.

Putting it all together, the first quote of the first line reads as follows: The June Live Cattle futures contract is currently trading at $0.74½, up $0.01. Therefore, you also need to know how each contract is quoted before you can interpret a price quote.

Grain:

Abbreviations

W	Wheat	Dollars per bushel
C	Corn	Dollars per bushel
O	Oats	Dollars per bushel
S	Soybeans	Dollars per bushel
SM	Soybean Meal	Dollars per ton
SO	Soybean Oil	Cents per pound

Meat:

LC	Live Cattle	Cents per pound
FC	Feeder Cattle	Cents per pound
LH	Live Hogs	Cents per pound
PB	Pork Bellies	Cents per pound

Energy:

HO	NY Heating Oil	Cents per gallon
HV	NY Unleaded Gas	Cents per gallon
CL	Light Crude Petroleum	Dollars per barrel

Physical Commodity Market Specifications

Commodity	Exch	Trading Hrs Central Time	Delivery Months	Contract Size	Price Quote	Pt. Value Fluctuation	Min. Price	Daily Limits	
Cattle, Fdr.	CME	8:45- 1:00	F,H,J,K,Q,U,V,X	44,000 lbs	$/cwt	1pt =$4.40	2.5pts =$11.00	1.5¢=$660=150pts	
Cattle, Live	CME	8:45- 1:00	G,J,M,Q,V,Z	40,000 lbs	$/cwt	1pt =$4.00	2.5pts =$10.00	1.5¢=$600=150pts	
Cattle, Live	MA	8:45- 1:15	G,J,M,Q,V,Z	20,000 lbs	$/cwt	1pt =$2.00	2.5pts =$5.00	1.5¢=$300=150pts	
Cocoa (Metric)	NYCSCE	8:30- 1:15	H,K,N,Z	10M ton (22,046)	$/M ton	1pt =$10.00	1pt =$10.00	$880=88pts(1)	
Coffee "C"	NYCSCE	8:15- 12:58	H,K,N,U,Z	37,500 lbs	¢/lb	1pt =$3.75	5pts =$18.75	6¢/600pts(1)	
Copper, High Grade	COMEX	8:25- 1:00	F,H,K,N,U,Z	25,000 lbs	¢/lb	1pt =$2.50	5pt =$12.50	None	
Corn	CBOT	8:30- 1:15	H,K,N,U,Z	5,000 bu	¢/bu	1¢ =$50.00	1/4¢ =$12.50	12¢=$600(5)	
Corn	MA	8:30- 1:45	H,K,N,U,Z	1,000 bu	¢/bu	1¢ =$10.00	1/8¢ =$1.25	12¢=$120	
Cotton	NYCTE	9:30- 1:40	H,K,N,V,Z	50,000 lbs	¢/lb	1pt =$5.00	1pt =$5.00	2¢/200pts(4)	
Crude Oil	NYME	8:45- 2:10	All Months	1,000 barrels	$/barrel	1pt =$10.00	1pt =$10.00	(7)	
Gasoline, Unleaded	NYME	8:50- 2:10	All Months	42,000 gal	¢/gal	1pt =$4.20	1pt =$4.20	(6)	
Gold	CBOT	7:20- 1:30	G,J,M,Q,V,Z	32.15 troy oz	$/oz	10¢ =$3.215	10¢ =$3.215	$50/t. oz=$1,607.50	
Gold	COMEX	7:20- 1:30	G,J,M,Q,V,Z	100 troy oz	$/oz	1pt =$1.00	10pts =$10.00	None	
Gold	MA	7:20- 1:40	F,H,J,M,N,U,V,Z	33.2 troy oz	$/oz	1pt =$.33	10 pts =$3.32	None	
Heating Oil	NYME	8:50- 2:10	All Months	42,000 gal	¢/gal	1pt =$4.20	1pt =$4.20	(6)	
Hogs	CME	9:10- 1:00	G,J,M,N,Q,V,Z	40,000 lbs	$/cwt	1pt =$4.00	2.5pts =$10.00	1.5¢=$600=150pts	
Hogs	MA	9:10- 1:15	G,J,M,N,Q,V,Z	20,000 lbs	$/cwt	1pt =$2.00	2.5pts =$5.00	1.5¢=$300=150pts	
Lumber	CME	9:00- 1:05	F,H,K,N,U,Z	160,000 bd ft	$/m/bd ft	1pt =$1.60	10pts =$16.00	$5/500pts(6)	
Natural Gas	NYME	8:20- 2:10	All Months	10,000 MMBtu	$/MMBtu	1pt =$10.00	1pt =$10.00	10¢=$1000=100pts	
Oats	CBOT	8:30- 1:15	H,K,N,U,Z	5,000 bu	¢/bu	1¢ =$50.00	1/4¢ =$12.50	10¢=$500(5)	
Oats	MA	8:30- 1:45	H,K,N,U,Z	1,000 bu	¢/bu	1¢ =$10.00	1/8¢ =$1.25	10¢=$100	
Orange Juice	NYCTE	9:15- 1:15	F,H,K,N,U,X	15,000 lbs	¢/lb	1pt =$1.50	5pts =$7.50	5¢=$750=500pts(2)	
Palladium	NYME	7:10- 1:20	H,M,U,Z	100 troy oz	$/oz	1pt =$1.00	5pts =$5.00	$6/600pts(3)	
Platinum	NYME	7:20- 1:30	F,J,N,V	50 troy oz	$/oz	1pt =$.50	10 pts =$5.00	$25/2500pts(3)	
Pork Bellies	CME	8:45- 1:00	G,H,K,N,Q	40,000 lbs	¢/lb	1pt =$4.00	2.5pts =$10.00	2¢=$800=200pts	

Table continues

Physical Commodity Market Specifications (Continued)

			All Months	42,000 gal	$/gal	1pt =$4.20	1pt =$4.20	4¢=$1680=400pts
Propane	NYME	8:15- 2:10	All Months	42,000 gal	$/gal	1pt =$4.20	1pt =$4.20	4¢=$1680=400pts
Rough Rice	MA	9:15- 1:30	F,H,K,N,U,X	200,000 lbs	¢/cwt	1pt =$2.00	5pts =$10.00	30¢=$600(5)
Silver	COMEX	7:25- 1:25	F,H,K,N,U,Z	5,000 troy oz	¢/oz	1pt =$ .50	50pts =$25.00	None
Silver, New	CBOT	7:25- 1:25	G,J,M,Q,V,Z	1,000 troy oz	¢/oz	1pt =$ .10	10 pts =$1.00	$1.00=$1000(3)
Silver	MA	7:25- 1:40	G,J,M,Q,V,Z	1,000 oz	¢/oz	1pt =$ .10	10 pts =$1.00	None
Soybean Meal	CBOT	8:30- 1:15	F,H,K,N,Q,U,V,Z	100 tons	$/ton	1pt =$1.00	10 pts =$10.00	$10/1000pts(5)
Soybean Oil	CBOT	8:30- 1:15	F,H,K,N,Q,U,V,Z	60,000 lbs	¢/lb	1pt =$6.00	1pt =$6.00	1¢/100pts(5)
Soybeans	CBOT	8:30- 1:15	F,H,K,N,Q,U,X	5,000 bu	¢/bu	1pt -$50.00	1/4¢= $12.50	30¢=$1500(5)
Soybeans	MA	8:30- 1:15	F,H,K,N,Q,U,X	1,000 bu	¢/bu	1pt =$10.00	1/8¢=$1.25	30¢=$300
Sugar	NYCSCE	9:00- 12:43	F,H,K,N,U,V	112,000 lbs	¢/lb	1pt =$11.20	1pt =$11.20	1/2¢/50pts(1)
Wheat	CBOT	8:30- 1:15	H,K,N,U,Z	5,000 bu	¢/bu	1¢=$50.00	1/4¢= $12.50	20¢=$1000(5)
Wheat	KCBT	8:30- 1:15	H,K,N,U,Z	5,000 bu	¢/bu	1¢=$50.00	1/4¢=$12.50	25¢=$1250
Wheat	MPLS	8:30- 1:45	H,K,N,U,Z	5,000 bu	¢/bu	1¢=$50.00	1/4¢= $12.50	20¢=$1000
Wheat	MA	8:30- 1:45	H,K,N,U,Z	1,000 bu	¢/bu	1¢=$10.00	1/8¢=$1.25	20¢=$200

Exchanges:

CBOT =Chicago Board of Trade
CME =Chicago Mercantile Exchange
COMEX =Commodity Exchange, Inc.(NY)
IMM =International Monetary Market (Div. of CME)
KCBT =Kansas City Board of Trade

MA =Mid America Commodity Exchange
MPLS =Minneapolis Board of Trade
NYCSCE =New York Coffee, Sugar and Cocoa Exchange
NYCTE =New York Cotton Exchange
NYME =New York Mercantile Exchange

Footnotes:

(1) No limits front two months
(2) Contact your broker for updated information.
(3) No limits front month.
(4) No limits after first Notice Day.
(5) No limits starting day before first Notice Day.
(6) Initial limit for front two months =2000 pts.   Total limit =4000 pts.   Back months initial limit =200 pts.   Total limit =2000 pts.
(7) Initial limit front two months =750 pts. Total limit =1500 pts. Back months initial limit =100 pts. Total limit =750 pts.

The information contained in this table is from sources believed to be reliable, but we cannot be held responsible for either its accuracy or completeness. All contract specifications are subject to change by action of the respective commodity exchange. Therefore, the specifications can be changed, sometimes without notice. You need to be in touch with your broker before entering any trade. Limits are subject to change and to variable limit rules of the respective exchange.

Food/Fiber:

Abbreviations

LB	Lumber	Dollars per 1000 bd. ft.
KC	Coffee	Cents per pound
CC	Cocoa	Dollars per ton
SB	Sugar	Cents per pound
CT	Cotton	Cents per pound
OJ	Orange Juice	Cents per pound

Metals:

SL	Silver	Dollars per ounce
GC	Gold	Dollars per ounce
HG	Copper	Cents per pound
PL	Platinum	Cents per pound
PA	Palladium	Cents per pound
AL	Aluminum	Cents per pound

With all this information—plus the data that follows—you should be able to work your way through most any quote system. Let's give it a try. You see the following stream across the bottom of your favorite cable TV financial program:

C 242 Z   HV 6600 M   CT 8325 V

What would this tell you? December corn is currently trading at $2.42 per bushel; June New York Unleaded Gas $0.66 per gallon; and October cotton is worth $0.83 1/4 per pound.

Worksheet 1

1. You are trading live cattle on the Chicago Mercantile Exchange. You bought one futures contract at $0.65 per pound and offset at $0.70. How much did you make or lose on this trade?

A. $1,000.00

B. $2,000.00

C. $3,000.00

D. $4,000.00

2. You are trading cotton. You shorted the market. When you offset your position, you lost six points on the trade. How much money did you lose?

A. $5.50

B. $25.00

C. $30.00

D. $300.00

3. As a Midwestern farmer, you feel you have a good fix on the direction of corn prices. You believe they are headed higher. Therefore, you go long five CBOT May corn contracts at $2.50. You offset your positions at $3.50. How did you do?

A. Lost $5,000.00

B. Gained $5,000.00

C. Lost $25,000.00

D. Gained $25,000.00

4. You are a silver bug, but you think it is headed for new, all-time lows. You load up on silver going short five January contracts of COMEX at $5.32. Unfortunately, silver heads north and you close out your position at $5.49. Your account will be:

A. Debited $850.00

B. Credited $850.00

C. Debited $4,250.00

D. Credited $4,250.00

Answers to Worksheet 1

1. The answer is B. A $0.05 profit was made. The CME live cattle contract calls for 40,000 pounds. Therefore, $0.05 × 40,000 lbs. equals $2,000.00.

2. The answer is C. One point in the cotton market equals $5.00. Therefore, six points would be a $30.00 loss.

3. The answer is D. For every $0.01 change in the corn price, the contract increases or decreases by $50.00. Since you were long and it gained $1.00, you would have made $5,000.00 per contract. Since you had five corn contracts, you profited $25,000 on the trade before paying transaction costs.

4. The answer is C. You were on the wrong side of a $0.17 silver move, from $5.32 to $5.49. On COMEX, your contract is for 5,000 troy ounces of silver. Therefore, each penny move equates to a $50.00 change—up or down. Since silver moved $0.17, each contract changed $850.00. You had five contracts which means a $4,250.00 loss. You were bearish during a bull rally.

2

Understanding Trading Strategies

Key Concepts

◆ There are four basic trading strategies to master—net position, hedging, option, and spread trading.

◆ Why you should seriously consider spread trading in the beginning.

◆ Understanding the four basic types of spreads.

◆ How to calculate gains or losses from spreads.

◆ Some actual spread examples.

There are four basic futures trading strategies. The first, and most common, is trading net long or net short positions. If you go long, you expect the market you're trading to move higher. You buy a commodity futures contract at a certain price and expect to sell (offset) it at a higher price. Trading net short is just the opposite. You're anticipating prices to go lower. You sell a commodity futures contract at a specified price and expect to buy it back at a lower price. Several examples of this strategy were given in the first chapter.

The second basic trading strategy is hedging, which is offsetting the price risk inherent in any commodity cash market by taking an opposite position in the same commodity futures market. The objective is to protect one's cash position from adverse price moves. For example, a farmer has 5,000 bushels of corn in a grain bin on his farm or growing in his fields. This makes him physically long one contract of corn. Let's say corn futures prices rise in June to a level that is attractive to the farmer, due to drought scares in other parts of the country or world. He knows his per bushel breakeven cost of production, say $1.80, and is satisfied with the profit margin included in the current December futures contract, say $2.30 or $0.50 per bushel or 27 percent gross profit margin. He can lock in this profit margin by immediately selling one futures contract on the Chicago Board of Trade.

By going short, he agrees to accept delivery of 5,000 bushels in December. When he harvests and delivers his corn to the local elevator, he offsets his commodity futures position. Although cash and futures prices have made many changes between June, when he went short, and November, when he delivered 5,000 bushels to the elevator, his profit margin stays approximately the same from the time that he entered the hedge. The only variations are the transaction costs (brokerage commission, fees, and interest on his margin money) required to execute the hedge.

We are not going to teach hedging in this text, but we need to call your attention to it for three specific reasons. First, hedgers can exert a great amount of influence on certain markets—driving prices higher or lower. Major grain companies, for example, can secretly negotiate sales of millions and millions of bushels of corn or wheat to countries like China or an Eastern block country. Before news of these sales become public, the grain company or the buying country may enter the commodity futures market. Major price rallies are often the first public indication a big sale is imminent, or has been consummated. Grains are not the only commodity hedged. Gold, silver, lumber, etc. are also commonly hedged.

The second reason you need to be aware of hedgers is that they have "strong hands." This means they will hold on to a position more tenaciously than most speculators. Hedgers have a legitimate business use for the commodity they trade. They need it, in most cases, to keep their business running or profitable. This means they will hold on to their positions through minor rallies or retracements. It often takes a major trend change to dislodge them. Speculators are a much more nervous breed and are much quicker to abandon a position once it becomes unprofitable.

There are reports periodically published within the industry to give you the position of the large traders, small traders, and hedgers. It pays to check these reports when you spot inexplicable price trends or patterns. This is the type of help you can expect from a good broker.

The third reason you need to know about hedgers is that there aren't the restrictions regarding trading insider information in the futures market that there are on the stock market. A broker can't give his orders a higher priority than his customers' orders if he trades for his own account. But any information—fact or fiction—learned about why a contract is going up or down can be traded, thus the LaSalle Street axiom: "Buy the rumor, sell the fact." This means when you hear a story that should move the market, a big grain sale to a foreign country for example, you buy the market. Once the rumor becomes fact, you reverse or offset your position because facts are usually more conservative or less exaggerated than rumors, and the market retraces.

The third basic trading strategy is options-on-futures. These are sometimes referred to as exchange traded options because they are traded on a government regulated exchange. They should not be confused with dealer options that are available in some commodities, like silver. Dealer options are not federally regulated, nor are they traded on exchanges. Nor should they be confused with stock options.

We do not have room for a detailed discussion of options, but we'll explain it briefly so you are aware of it as an alternative or adjunct to commodity trading.

When you purchase an option-on-futures or an exchange traded option, you obtain the right to assume a position in the commodity futures market. If you buy a call you have the right, but not the obligation, to take a long position in the futures market at a specific price, called the strike price. A put option gives you the right, but not the obligation, to take a short position in the futures market at a strike price.

Options have more or less risk than futures, depending on how you evaluate them. Brokers who sell options often emphasize the controlled or defined nature of the risk associated with buying options. When you buy an option, you pay the seller of the option a premium. Along with the premium, you pay the transaction costs. These include the broker's commission and fees to the National Futures Association, the exchange, and the firm that clears (physically executes) the trade. The clearing firm is called an FCM (Futures Commission Merchant).

Options are classified as wasting assets. This means that after a specific amount of time, from a few days to several months, or even a year or more, they expire. The closer they get to expiration, the less their time value is worth. When they eventually expire, they are worthless. You lose 100 percent of your investment (premium and transaction costs) at this time. This aspect of the risk nature of options comes into focus when you realize the vast majority of options expire worthless.

You make profits, or reduce the amount you lose on options, by offsetting them on the options market before they expire, just the same way you offset a futures position. Or, you can exercise the option, converting your option to a futures position. Then you trade the futures position as you normally would.

We only mention option trading because it is an alternative trading strategy you should be aware of before deciding how you are going to proceed in your investment in commodities. The last basic strategy to consider is spread trading.

Spread Trading

We think it is advantageous to discuss this topic in detail. Spread trading has certain advantages you should seriously consider when deciding which trading strategy is right for you. Additionally, there are certain spreads that are particularly apropos for the novice trader.

Spreading simply means you are simultaneously long (buying) and short (selling) related futures contracts. You are expecting one of the contracts to move farther or faster than the other—thus narrowing or widening the price spread between them. A spread trader profits by anticipating this change.

When do you use a spread? There are two classic spread opportunities. The first appears to be obvious—namely, when the prices of two commodity futures contracts are out-of-line, particularly if they are substantially so.

Take July wheat as an example. The Kansas City price is usually within a few cents of the Minneapolis price. Both markets are basically inland with similar transportation routes to the major cash markets. Let's say a spread trader notices a gap developing. It gets wider and wider, until there is over a dime difference— Minneapolis is trading at a premium to Kansas City.

What should the spread trader do? As with any other trade, the trader needs to understand what's causing the discrepancy. To do this, a firm understanding of the market is required. The wheat in Kansas City, for example, is hard red. It has a high protein content with a lot of gluten, making it ideal for bread. The northern wheat is durum, ideal for pasta.

When a situation like this occurred several years ago, the cause was bad crop news in Italy. Grain dealers in that country ran the price of durum wheat through the ceiling. In other words, there was a legitimate, fundamental reason for the widening of this price gap. The two markets were not working in tandem—hard red, in this case, is not a substitute for durum when it comes to pasta.

A true spread opportunity exists when there is an interrelationship between the commodities being spread. If they are moving independently, they should be traded that way. For a spread to work, the contracts should be influenced by the same fundamental forces so they expand and contract somewhat in unison. Otherwise one leg will get completely out of position and this could be expensive. If this happens, you can offset the losing leg and hold the profitable one, but you are no longer spread trading when this occurs. It is also a high risk play and violates one of our trading rules, described in Chapter 8.

The second important spread trading opportunity occurs when there are major shifts taking place in the market place. A classic example is the old crop-new crop shift. As harvest approaches, if traders think there will be a strong demand before the new crop is harvested, the spread traders go long the nearby (old crop) and short the distant (new crop). This is a bull spread. If, on the other hand, traders decide demand going into harvest will be weak, they'll short the nearby and buy the more distant contracts, or bear spread the market.

The shifts in supply and demand that take place in specific markets can often be attributed to seasonal changes. If a seasonal pattern can be predicted and is dependable, it provides an excellent spread opportunity.

Why use a spread? Couldn't you have just as easily held simple long or short positions? The answer is risk management. Take the bull spread as an example. If your analysis is wrong and the corn market declines before the new crop is harvested, your short of the new crop would have gained in value. But, it probably would not have gained as much as the long of the new crop contract lost. On the other hand, you would not have lost as much as if you were holding only net long positions in either the old or the new crop.

Additionally, the margin money required is lower. This increases your leverage, or the efficient use of your trading equity. You can earn just as high a percentage of profit as you would with a net long or short position.

But please do not consider spreading a risk-free commodity futures trade—none exist! To be successful, you must have a firm understanding of all the factors influencing the specific spread you're considering. What will be the impact of the seasonal patterns? Carryover? Technical chart patterns? Market psychology? Pipeline supplies? Spread trading, like any other trading, requires sound market analysis, discussed in the next chapter.

Another important consideration is leverage. The margin requirement for a spread is generally about 60 percent of what would be charged to trade both legs separately. For example, let's say you're considering a wheat/corn spread. Separately, the margin for wheat might be $750.00 per contract and $500.00 for corn, a total of $1,250.00. The margin for these two contracts traded as a spread might only be $750.00. Brokerage commissions are usually less, too, when compared to trading two separate futures contracts, but higher than trading one outright position.

Types of Spreads

There are four basic types of spreads:

1. **Interdelivery or intracommodity spread:**
   Futures contracts for the same commodities are traded on the same exchange and are spread between two different delivery months. For example, CBOT July wheat is spread against CBOT December wheat.

2. **Intermarket spread:**
   Commodity contracts for the same commodity deliverable in the same month are spread between two different commodity exchanges. For example, Chicago September silver is spread against New York September silver or London silver.

3. **Intercommodity spread:**
   Futures contracts traded on the same exchange for the same delivery month are spread between two different commodities that are substitutable for each other in some uses. For example, March CBOT corn is spread against March CBOT oats, both of which are used to feed livestock and poultry.

4. **Commodity-product spread:**
   Futures contracts are spread between a commodity and the product or products derived from that commodity, and are traded on the same exchange. The most common spread of this type is soybeans versus soybean oil and meal, called the Soybean Crush Spread. Another common one is crude oil versus gasoline and heating oil spread, which is called the Crack Spread.

Let's look at each of these in turn.

The Interdelivery Spread

These are usually intracommodity spreads, or spreads made within the same commodity but between different delivery months. The specific example we'll be discussing is the July/November Soybean Spread.

The first fact you need to know about this spread is that the soybean crop year begins on September 1 and ends on August 31 each year. In other words, the spread is between two crop years. July represents the last major old crop marketing month, and November is the first major new crop marketing month. Although we are talking about two crop years, the delivery months of the spread are in the same calendar year.

Next, you need to know about the historical price patterns. Prices for agricultural commodities tend to make their lows during harvest (November) and then trend higher as the marketing year progresses. There are two reasons for this. First, the price normally increases as the carrying costs increase. Carrying costs are the expenses—storage, interest, spoilage, insurance—attributed to holding or "carrying the crop" until it is sold.

The second, and a more important factor, is the supply-demand equation. Supplies are plentiful at harvest, therefore, prices are lower. As the supply diminishes and gets tighter, prices usually respond by moving higher. If there are any abnormalities such as a weather scare at planting, a summer drought, higher than expected yields or acreage planted, the spread widens or narrows. The spread trader must anticipate whether the old or new crop will be affected more, and in what direction.

These historical patterns are not as dependable as they once were, since the introduction of the South American factor. Argentina and Brazil have opened enormous amounts of cropland to soybean production over the last 20 years. They plant when we harvest; harvest when we plant. This means their crop is available to world markets when our crop is supposed to be making highs.

Historically in this country, July soybeans in one crop year are priced higher than November soybeans of the following crop year. To calculate the spread, you subtract November futures prices from the July. This generally gives you a positive number. For example, if July beans are trading at $5.50 and November at $5.36, the spread would be $0.14.

The spread trader must next decide which way the spread is headed. Will it widen or become more narrow? The key factor is the quantity of soybeans that will be carried over from one year to the next. This links the two contracts, causing them to move up and down together.

The formula for calculating total supplies is simple. You add the current year's production to last year's carryover. From this figure, you subtract the current year's expected total usage to get the anticipated amount to be carried over into the next crop year. You must also subtract any soybeans tied up in any government controlled programs, if any are in effect, plus beans held back for use as seed.

The final authority on soybean stocks, usage, production, and carryover is the United States Department of Agriculture (USDA). They publish periodic progress reports, including carryover tables. There are also several private consultants and forecasting firms that project these figures. Traders use these numbers, plus other fundamental and technical factors, in their analysis.

If these reports indicate a decline in carryover, pressure builds on the old crop as supplies tighten. This drives old crop prices higher. The spread narrows, since the new crop is not affected as much. New crop prices usually increase when old crop prices do, but at a slower rate.

How wide can the July/November soybean spread become? There's really no limit. In 1973, the spread exceeded $5.00 and a spread of $1.00 or more is not uncommon.

Conversely, when demand falls or production increases, carryover increases and prices decline. When this occurs, July contracts fall faster and farther than November contracts. The spread narrows. How narrow can it get? In years of extremely weak demand, old crop prices can fall below new crop, producing a negative spread. This means July futures contracts are trading at a discount to November. Keep in mind the carrying cost mentioned earlier. These costs must be paid each month on the old crop, yet the new crop, without any of these charges, is higher. Since the old crop can be carried to the time the new crop is available for delivery, this tends to put a limit on the amount the spread can narrow.

Changes in supply can cause even more dramatic changes in the spread. For example, if there is the anticipation of a large crop during the growing season, November prices may fall. This may drive July prices down as well, if users defer purchases until after harvest. July prices may fall so much the spread narrows. On the other hand, if reduced acreage or weather problems reduce supplies, July prices may climb faster than November, narrowing the spread. In this case, users are scrambling to assure themselves of an adequate supply. Other factors, like government actions, imports, exports, world conditions, and yields can also produce changes in the spread.

How do you profit from the spread? If you expect the spread to widen, you can buy July futures contracts and sell November. Or, if you believe the spread will narrow, you sell July beans and buy November beans simultaneously.

Both sides or legs of the spread are executed at the same time. There are brokers in the pits who specialize in the most popular spreads and handle the entire transaction as a unit.

The Intermarket Spread

At the beginning of this chapter we discussed the July wheat spread between the Kansas City and Minneapolis exchanges. This is an intermarket spread. The risk the trader faces is local pressure or unique characteristics (bread vs. pasta) of one of the legs of the spread. Otherwise, this spread works the same way the intradelivery spread does.

The Intercommodity Spread

Now, let's take a look at the wheat/corn spread. The first question a spread trader resolves is the relationship—in this case both can be used for food and animal feed. But, as you may remember, you need to do some research to make sure there aren't some unusual circumstances impacting one leg of this spread that are totally unrelated to the other.

Next, you want to determine if the relationship between the two commodities is normal by historical standards. After that, you need to decide if you expect the difference (spread) between the two to expand or contract.

Studying wheat and corn, you should look at the seasonal price patterns first. Corn is planted in the spring and harvested in the fall. Prices seasonally are lowest at harvest time and usually make highs in late summer. Wheat is divided between winter and spring varieties, based on when it's planted. Harvesting takes place in May-June and late summer, respectively. Therefore, the price is usually lowest from late May through summer because of harvest pressures. The highs are commonly posted during the winter months.

If you were to trade the wheat/corn spread using the seasonal patterns, you might expect the spread to narrow sometime in May, June, or July. Wheat prices, which are normally higher than corn, are weak—heading down as the harvest unfolds. Corn prices are moving up in response to reduced inventory and weather worries.

This means the spread should close in May, June and July—wheat prices coming down and corn prices going up. It widens during September, October, and November—wheat prices heading north and corn moving south as the harvest gets into full swing.

Here's a specific example to study.

It is May 18, 1988. Corn is trading for $2.20 per bushel and wheat is at $3.30. This gives us a $1.10 spread. We expect the spread to narrow and are in a bull spread. By the middle of July, corn limits up a few days and is trading at $3.40. Wheat is at $4.00. The spread is now $0.60. We have made a $0.50 profit or $2,500.00 before transaction costs.

You calculate it like this:

Wheat

Initial Position Short Wheat:		$4.40
Offset Position Long Wheat		$4.00
	Loss	($0.70)

Corn

Initial Position Long Corn:		$2.20
Offset Position Short Corn		$3.40
	Profit $	1.20

Combining Positions (Profit minus Loss) $1.20 − $0.70 = $0.50

Net profit per bushel times 5,000 bushels per contract equals $2,500.00.

On the high side, your transaction costs could be approximately $200.00, giving you a net gain of $2,300.00. If you divide this by a margin of $750.00, your return to margin is over 300 percent. Another way to look at it is: How much does the spread have to move to break even? If your transaction costs are $200.00, the spread would have to move $0.04. Anything beyond that is your profit.

The Commodity-Product Spread

The classic commodity-product spread is the Soybean Crush Spread. Soybeans are processed into meal and oil. Therefore, to put on the Crush Spread, you can buy (or sell) soybean commodity futures and sell (or buy) its by-products, namely the soybean oil and soybean meal commodity futures contracts.

The crush spread is quoted as the difference between the combined sale value of the meal and oil, and the price of the beans. But this creates a small problem. Beans are quoted in cents per bushel, meal in dollars per ton and oil in cents per pound. Therefore, you need to convert the meal and oil prices to cents per bushel to match up with the beans.

The crush spread is based on a bushel of soybeans weighing 60 pounds. This would produce 48 pounds of meal and 11 pounds of oil. This totals 59 pounds with the one missing pound being lost in the production process.

To convert the meal, you divide the 48-pound meal yield by 2,000 pounds, a ton. This gives you a conversion factor of .024. Multiply this times the price of meal gives you the cents, or dollars and cents, per bushel. For example, if meal is at $176.00 per ton, multiply this by .024 equals $4.22 per bushel.

Oil is a little simpler. If the current futures price of soybean oil is $.19 1/4 per pound, the 11 pounds in the bushel of beans would be worth $2.12.

Now that all three components of the crush spread have been converted to dollars and cents per one bushel, we can calculate the gross processing margin (GPM). That's the difference between the combined sales value of the by-products (meal and oil) and the cost of the input (soybeans). Does it pay to crush soybeans? Is there enough of a profit margin to pay for the processing plus a reasonable profit for the crusher?

In our example, the combined sales value of the meal and oil is $6.34. If soybeans are trading at $5.50 per bushel, GPM would be $0.84. There is no iron-clad rule, but most industry sources agree that a minimum of a $0.15 GPM is required to crush. The $0.84 in our example is on the high side of the historical figures.

The next question the crush trader confronts is whether the spread will narrow or widen. Let's assume traders anticipate the spread to narrow. The price of soybeans is expected to gain on the value of the meal and oil due to drought conditions in the Midwest, as an example. With this scenario, the traders would "put on the crush" by buying beans and selling meal and oil. On the other hand, some traders may believe the GPM is going to widen. They anticipate cooler temperatures and abundant rain to break the drought. Soybeans would lose ground to meal and oil. In this case, these traders could "put on the reverse crush" by selling beans and buying meal and oil.

In either instance, the spread could be put on in a one-to-one-to-one contract ratio, namely one or an equal number of each contract, or it could be traded as a "crush package." With the package, you bid the crush or reverse crush by offering a particular GPM. There are floor brokers who specialize in trading crush packages and handle all three legs of the spread at one time.

The package is usually based on 10 soybeans, 12 soybean meal, and nine soybean oil contracts. This ratio approximates the equivalent yields of meal and oil from a bushel of soybeans more accurately than the one-to-one-to-one ratio.

Determining whether the GPM will narrow or widen can be tricky. The reason is simply that you're dealing with three related commodities, yet all three are sometimes influenced by the same factors and at other times by totally unrelated factors. For example, if the dollar is weak, the world markets clamber for all three—beans, oil, and meal. On the other hand, if the dollar is strong, the export demand would be reduced for oil, but the domestic demand for meal could still be strong.

Interest rates also impact the spread. When they are high and going higher, soybean users will attempt to keep inventories at a minimum. This usually reduces bean demand, causing the spread to widen.

Soybean oil often marches to its own drummer as it competes with other oils—sunflower, palm, coconut, rapeseed, etc.—on a worldwide basis. Often the strength or weakness of the soybean oil market is totally unrelated to beans and meal. At other times, abundant soybean oil stocks can narrow the GPM, while shortages will widen it.

Demand for meal alone can sometimes control the direction of the GPM. This is referred to in the trade as the "crush for meal" syndrome. Livestock numbers are usually expanding at a very fast pace and gobbling up all the meal that can be produced. As with any crop-based spread, weather is also critical. Export demand and carryover are also important. Successful crush traders know their seasonal and cyclical patterns inside out, and keep a close eye on all USDA planting and usage reports.

Your selection of a trading strategy is a critical issue. It must be one you are comfortable with and have a high degree of confidence in. This decision can also affect the broker you hire. Some account executives specialize in options or spread trading, while others can provide whatever assistance you need.

Our best advice is to put your thoughts in writing. What strategy really appeals to you? Why? Do you have any special interests or expertise that would make you more at home with one strategy as opposed to another? Then ask probing questions of prospective brokers to find one who can satisfy your needs.

Worksheet 2

1. What are the four basic trading strategies?

    A. _____

    B. _____

    C. _____

    D. _____

2. As a commodity speculator, you are concerned about what hedgers do because:

   A. They can't make up their minds, causing trendless markets.

   B. There's no reason to pay any attention to them because they have no influence on the markets.

   C. They can have a major impact on prices.

3. "Buy the rumor, sell the fact" means?

   A. There is a commodity market in news stories.

   B. Rumors often exaggerate the fact, resulting in wildly moving markets that subside once the facts become known.

   C. Just about anything will stampede commodity brokers.

4. If you buy an exchange-traded option, you:

   A. Must convert it at some time to a commodity position.

   B. Take on less risk than owning an outright commodity futures position.

   C. It will eventually expire worthless if it isn't offset or exercised.

5. Spread trading entails:

   A. Holding a long and short position in two unrelated markets.

   B. All the advantages of futures trading with none of the risk.

   C. Holding equal, but opposite, positions in interrelated futures contracts.

6. What are the four basic types of spreads?

   A. _____

   B. _____

   C. _____

   D. _____

7. What is the most common or classical use of the intracommodity spread?

   A. Spread between old and new crop.

   B. Corn and soybeans.

C. To make money in futures trading.

8. Before entering a spread, what are the three factors you should immediately check?

A. _____

B. _____

C. _____

9. How do you calculate the profit or loss of a spread?

A. After offsetting both legs, you calculate the gain or loss on each separately, and them combine them.

B. You multiply the change that has taken place by the number of units of the commodity being spread times the number of contracts in each leg.

C. You check with an electronic futures price quotation service.

Answers to Worksheet 2

1. The four basic futures trading strategies are:

A. Trading net long or net short

B. Hedging

C. Trading options-on-futures or exchange traded options

D. Spread trading

2. The answer is C. Hedges often have a very strong influence on the trend of futures price. It is because they have a real need or use for the commodities they hedge. This means they trade for the long run and do not easily relinquish their positions.

3. The answer is B.

4. The answer is C. All options eventually expire worthless if not offset or exercised. Exercised means conversion to the underlying commodity futures contracts.

Regarding A, buying an options gives you the right, but not the obligation, to take a commodity futures position at a given (strike) price.

Answer B may have confused you. Buying options on futures is often considered or promoted as being less risky than owning an outright position in the commodity market. In our opinion, this is only partially true. It is true in the sense that, once you pay the premium and the transaction cost (brokerage commission and fees), you are not liable for anything additional. You do not face, as futures traders do, the possibility of margin calls. Unless, of course, you exercise the option and take a position in the commodity market.

On the other hand, you do face the very real possibility of losing 100 percent of your investment (the premium and transaction costs). This is very likely to happen since the overwhelming majority of options expire worthless.

5.   The answer is C. If the markets you are spreading are unrelated, it is the same as simply holding net long and net short positions. It is the fact that the markets being spread are related and will be influenced by the same factors that modifies the risk. But there is always risk when speculating in the futures market—never forget it.

6.   The four basic types of spreads are:

A.   Interdelivery Spread—Same commodity, same exchange, different delivery months.

B.   Intermarket Spread—Same commodity, same month, different exchange.

C.   Intercommodity Spread—Same exchange, same month, different commodities.

D.   Commodity–product Spread—Between a commodity and its by-products, or the reverse.

7.   The answer is A. "Intra," of course, means within. In this case, it is referring to being within the same commodity—same commodity, different delivery months. Another name for this type of spread is intercommodity. It is common to create a spread with one delivery month on either side of harvest for an agricultural commodity. There are often reasonably predictable seasonal price patterns that come into play.

8.   Before entering a spread, the first thing to do is make sure there is a real relationship between the contracts to be spread. Look for unusual circumstances that might impact the price of one leg and not the other.

Next, you must decide if the current price relation is normal or abnormal. Lastly, your analysis must determine if the spread will widen or become narrower. This determines whether you initiate a bull or a bear spread.

9.   The answer is A. With B, you can do it this way, but you must make sure that the difference is measured in the same unit as the price is calculated. For example, the tick price of corn is one-fourth of a cent and the contract is evaluated in dollars and cents per bushel. Therefore, if you multiplied the difference in ticks times 5,000 bushels in the contract, you would not get the right price.

3

Market Analysis

Key Concepts

◆ The pros and cons of fundamental and technical analysis.

◆ How to forecast commodity price trends.

◆ Understanding the five basic types of technical analysis, i.e., bar chart analysis, trend following, structural, character-of-the-market, and miscellaneous approaches.

◆ Combining fundamental and technical analysis.

No matter which of the four basic trading strategies you plan to use to trade the commodity markets, you must decide how you are going to anticipate the next market move—will it be up, down, or sideways? Which techniques are you going to use to analyze the markets? Which markets will you attempt to analyze? These questions go hand in hand.

Fundamental Approach

Market analysis falls into two general categories—fundamental and technical. Fundamental analysis is based on the theory that the price of a commodity at any given time is the equilibrium point between supply and demand. Technical analysis is based on the theory that price directions and moves can be determined solely from an analysis of price and other statistical data.

Which markets to trade? You want to make this decision at the same time you decide what analytical method or methods you'll be using, because they are closely intertwined. Traders, particularly new traders, are more comfortable analyzing a market they understand.

This is particularly important with fundamental analysis. Fundamentalists must take every possible contingency into consideration. Therefore, these traders must know their commodity(ies) inside out.

In theory, fundamental analysis sounds simple. All you do is add whatever is left over from last year to this year's production and subtract this year's usage. The formula is: Carryover plus production (supply) less usage (demand) equals available stocks. From this figure, price projections can be made.

In practice, it is anything but simple. Carryover may be stored in places where it is difficult or impossible to measure—on farms in remote parts of the world or in uncooperative countries. Carryover needs to be further defined as "usable" carryover. The old Soviet Empire historically grew enough food to feed itself, but so much got spoiled there was never enough to go around. Also, moving the carryover to where it is needed can pose such insurmountable problems it becomes impossible or impractical. Equally common is for the "have not" countries to lack the money to buy from the "have plenty" countries.

Production is even trickier, especially for the agricultural commodities. Think about the impact weather has on yields. Who can accurately forecast it? Then there are planting intentions to predict in the beginning of the year, pollination in the middle, and harvest at the end. For most crops, all this must be evaluated worldwide. Some countries deliberately distort and misguide analysts in an attempt to get an unfair advantage for their country. Others don't have the internal capabilities to make accurate predictions or evaluations, even if they wanted to.

So far, we've only discussed the supply side of these equations. Demand is equally difficult to quantify because it is often a function of price. The cheaper a commodity becomes, the more of it is used and new uses are found for it. When commodities become scarce and expensive, usage is cut down or substitute commodities are brought into the market place.

This is still only the tip of the fundamental analysis iceberg. Government regulation, policies, and interference can drastically alter either the supply or demand side of the equation. Or there must be taken into account the implementation of a new process that reduces demand, such as the development of digital photography that may reduce the use of silver in developing photographic negatives. Dock strikes and war can disrupt supply lines. Too much or too little inflation can totally negate what otherwise would be a meaningful analysis. The unexpected announcement of a new use for a standard commodity can send prices soaring, while cancellation of an important sale or marketing treaty can send prices south just as fast.

Everything that has been discussed so far applies to virtually all commodities, not just the agricultural ones. Think about all the political shenanigans that go on involving foreign currencies, precious metals, industrial metals, crude oil, orange juice, etc., etc.

How do you input all these factors into a supply-demand equation? This has always been one of the toughest challenges facing fundamentalists. The next is gathering, updating, and evaluating everything that can or could modify prices. Once this is accomplished, if at all possible, a value must be assigned to the input. For example, how many cents per bushel will corn be affected by a two-month drought in half the Midwest?

The hope for a solution to this dilemma was the computerization of a model taking "every" variable into consideration. Some of these models appear to work in normal years. A normal year is one in which nothing unexpected or unplanned occurs. Unfortunately, normal years are rare.

The bottom line for most traders is they can't afford the cost of developing a fundamental model, nor do they have the time and resources to perfect it and keep it current. On the other hand, in many markets, fundamental analysis can be very helpful to determine the long term trend. This is because there are certain commodities that can't make major trend changes abruptly.

Live cattle are an example. They have the following production cycle:

1. It takes 14 to 18 months from the time a heifer (female calf) is born until she can be bred.

2. Once bred, there is a nine-month gestation period before she delivers a calf.

3. It then takes approximately 17-19 months for a bull calf to reach slaughter weight.

That means it is over two and a half years from the time a cow is bred until a steak is produced from its offspring. In other words, livestock producers can't immediately jack up production when prices are attractively high. Likewise, they can't abruptly cut back production when prices are low without slaughtering the production system.

Gold and silver have similar production restrictions, but for other reasons. These precious metals are often mined as by-products of the production of base metals, such as lead and iron ore. As long as the base metals are being mined, some of the precious metals are brought to market. Unlike livestock, precious metals are not perishable and can be stored indefinitely, but with a carrying charge (storage, insurance, interest).

Therefore, fundamental analysis can often be used to get an overall understanding of what the long term trend is. If you're a hedger or a position trader, this is valuable information.

If you're a short term speculator, as most individual commodity traders are, it is good to be sensitive to the long term trend—but you can't trade it. This means you need another type of analysis that's more short term in nature. Most speculators rely on technical analysis for these and other reasons.

Technical Price Forecasting

Is technical analysis voodoo, or a self-fulfilling prophecy? It has been called both. In our opinion, those who don't trust it just don't realize there are some sound psychological reasons why it works. Before we go too far, we'd better start with some definitions. According to the National Futures Association's "Glossary of Futures Terms":

> Technical analysis—An approach to analysis of futures markets which examines patterns of price change, rates of change and changes in volume of trading, open interest and other statistical indicators. This data is often charted. See also Charting. (Page 22)

> Charting—The use of graphs and charts in the technical analysis of futures markets to plot price movements, volume, open interest or other statistical indicators of price movement. (Page 4)

Pure technicians totally disregard everything but the signals generated by their technical system. The theory is that every fundamental factor affecting supply and demand reflects in the price. Therefore, if you study the stream of prices flowing from the trading pits and the related statistics, such as volume, open interest, and momentum, you can uncover trends and anticipate future price objectives.

We divide technical analysis into five basic types—bar charts of prices, trend-following, structural, character-of-market, and "other." Price bar charting is probably the most common. Daily, weekly, and monthly prices are charted and the formations analyzed. An example of trend-following technical analysis is moving averages, which combines a series of prices and averages them mathematically. Structural analysis assumes the market moves in established, recognizable patterns—like seasonals, cyclical or wave patterns. Probably the most sophisticated is character-of-market. This type of analysis attempts to exactly measure the "quality" of a price movement, then takes a position opposite the momentum, anticipating where the market is headed next.

As you might guess, our last category, "other," is a collection for all types of analysis that are not easily classified. This could be anything from something as simple as trading contrary opinion to insights gained from studying the phases of the moon.

Later in this chapter, we'll discuss each type of analysis in a little more detail giving some specific examples. Now, though, we need to try and convince you that there is some validity to this approach.

Why Technical Analysis Works

The accusation made earlier, that technical analysis is a self-fulfilling prophecy, evolves from the fact that its use is so widely accepted. For example, one of the simplest techniques is drawing trendlines on price charts. The most common example of this is the up or down trendline. Every technical trader is taught that when a major trendline is broken, it's time to reverse one's positions. And, just like clock work, when prices break the trend, "all" the traders reverse their positions—fulfilling its prophecy. For this reason alone, anyone trading futures should know the basics of chart analysis, if nothing more than to anticipate what other traders can be expected to do.

One of the most compelling reasons for having faith in technical analysis is the enormous amount of trading equity controlled by technical traders. We have access to a database of over 100 professional commodity trading advisers managing hundreds of millions of dollars. Of this group, only a handful are solely fundamental traders. The vast majority use technical analysts of one sort or another. This, we think, is true throughout the industry.

The reason for this is simply the enormous amount of information required to trade successfully using fundamental analysis. The natural consequence of acquiring gigantic amounts of data is not having the time and resources to do the analysis. This makes the use of fundamental analysis almost prohibitive for the individual trader.

Another little quirk of fundamental analysis is that it is not self-correcting. For example, if a trendline is broken, or a support-resistance level penetrated, the technical trader views this as a reason to reverse or abandon a position. But what does the fundamental analyst think, if he thought corn was a good buy at $2.00 per bushel and it drops to $1.50? Is it a better buy? When does one reverse one's position? When do you "know" you're wrong?

Before we go too far, we want to stress the fact we are not belittling fundamental analysis in any way. There are major grain companies and well-known professional traders (CTAs) who use it as their primary analytic technique. It is also very common for all types of traders to use fundamental analysis to determine the basic trend or the overall direction of the market. Then, technical analysis is used to select specific exit and entry points.

Another problem with fundamental analysis is unknown factors. We have seen many unexpected political moves in recent years—the fall of the Berlin Wall, the Iraqi invasion of Kuwait, to name just two—that have sent the market reeling uncontrollably. How do fundamental traders handle these? Hopefully with protective stops.

Technical traders will see the market breaking a trendline or generating an exit signal of some sort, and react. Technicians have "reasons" to reverse or stand aside (not trade) the market(s).

Please don't get the impression technical analysis is a panacea. Traders can, unfortunately, lose money just as easily and just as fast with technical analysis as they do using fundamental analysis. The big difference is there are technical analysis systems that are manageable or controllable by small traders.

One thing we have learned over many years in futures trading is that it is not the system alone that generates success for traders. If there were one or two perfect systems, we'd all know about them and they probably wouldn't work any more. But there are hundreds and thousands of systems.

To make a system work, you must combine it with sound money management techniques and stick with it. By constantly fine-tuning a system, you can make it work for you. Your system's and your money management rules must make you a disciplined trader—one who can survive the inevitable losses you will sustain.

This brings us to the subject of the Law of Probability, one of the cornerstones of successful futures trading. Probability and survivability—you must understand these concepts and work them into your trading and money management systems.

To make money as a futures trader, you need three "rights." You must be in the right market, on the right side (bull or bear), and at the right time. To be right three times, you need to be extremely lucky, or you need to have patience.

Compare commodity trading to fly fishing. You repeatedly cast your fly where you think the trout are. If there isn't a fish where you cast your bait, you immediately retrieve it and try again. In essence, that's what commodity trading is all about. You constantly enter the markets. If the trade doesn't work, you close it out. If it does, you reel in the winnings. This old adage sums it all up: "Cut your losses short, let your winners run!"

To be able to cast and cast and cast until you get a strike, you need to be very disciplined. Solid money management rules, like "never risk more than 10% of your equity on one trade" or "always use protective stops," must be followed religiously. Without a system you are committed to and money management rules to follow, you have to rely on luck. If that's what you want to do, consider a lottery. (We'll discuss rules in more detail in Chapter 8.)

Chart Reading

Now let's get back to a discussion of the basic types of technical analysis. Commodity price bar charting services come in all sizes and shapes. Some are as large as a tabloid newspaper, making it easy to update between weekly issues and to draw trendlines and other signals. Others are small enough to fit in a vest pocket for easy access and portability.

The complexity of the additional statistical studies, aside from the basic charts included, varies widely. Most include volume and open interest. Some add several moving averages, stochastic, and even point and figure charts. Another important variable is the number of charts. You can get charting services covering just the metal markets or the agriculturals. Others track all major commodities and may include several different delivery months, or just the spot month. For some commodities, charts of the cash markets may be an important feature.

One charting service, for example, includes a composite index of all the physical commodities to assist traders in discerning overall trends. This composite index is broken into four sub-indexes—grains, meats, metals and food/fiber. By comparing the sub-indexes to each other and the composite index, you can see which group of commodities is pushing the market higher or tugging it lower. You can then select individual commodities to trade from the groups with the most momentum.

Naturally, the price of the various services reflects their degree of sophistication. They range from a low of $52.00 per year to a high of over $300.00. Most are weekly, but some services offer semiweekly and monthly editions.

The basic element of the price bar chart is the price tick (Figure 3-1). The vertical line represents the unit's (day, week, month) trading range. The top is the high and the bottom is the low. The short horizontal line on the left denotes the

Figure 3-1: Price Ticks

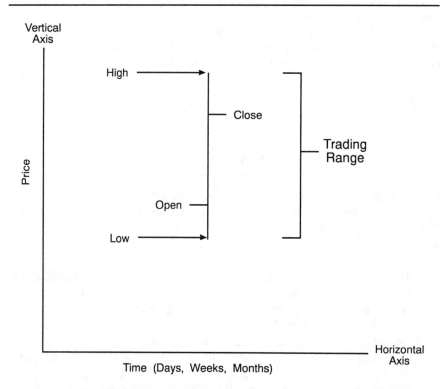

The Price Tick is the basic element of commodity price charts. The vertical line denotes the price range for the period (day, week, month). The left horizontal tick mark indicates the open, and the right horizontal tick the close.

opening prices and the one on the right (as you face it) is the close. Not all charts include the right or opening price tick. The vertical axis of the chart represents price and the horizontal time.

Daily, weekly, and monthly bar charts are depicted similarly with the high, low, and close represented by a vertical line above the date. Non-trading days, weekends, and holidays are not depicted, so there is no break in the pattern.

Long term charts, covering months and years of price activity, periodically show price distortions up or down. Careful analysis often reveals these are places where the contract rolled over from one contract month to the next. For example, the June silver contract expired and the chart service continued the chart using the December contract. In this case, there could be a price gap or distortion. The reason is simply that, as the June silver contract approached expiration or delivery, trading heated up driving prices a little higher or lower. The far out contract, December, may have been traded with less volatility and prices remained steady. Our point is that the roll-over from one contract to another can sometimes cause a distortion depending on the factors influencing the different delivery months. These longer term charts are often referred to as "continuation" charts.

As a rule, the longer term the chart, the smoother the pricing pattern becomes. This means that the price patterns on weekly charts are usually smoother than those on daily charts, and that monthly charts are smoother than weekly ones. Also, the longer the term of the chart, the more reliable the pattern is considered. For example, an area on a monthly chart that has given support to prices (we'll be discussing specific price patterns shortly) would be expected to be stronger (or more reliable) than the same formation on a weekly or daily chart. This is generally true for all formations or chart signals.

Across the bottom of most daily charting services (see Figure 3–2), you'll find a record of the trading volume and open interest for that day. Volume indicates the total number of contracts traded. Open interest measures the number of contracts held at the conclusion of a trading session. These are very important figures because they tell you the degree of activity of traders, or the momentum of the market you're studying. We'll be discussing these in more detail as we discuss specific price patterns.

Chart Formations

You could fill a good size bookcase with full-length texts discussing interpretations of bar charts. Several of the better ones have been cited in the bibliography. What

Figure 3–2: Daily Price Chart

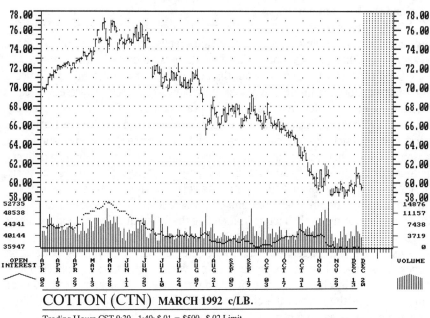

COTTON (CTN) MARCH 1992 c/LB.

Trading Hours CST 9:30 - 1:40; $.01 = $500 $.02 Limit

The basic tool used by most chartists is the Daily Futures Price Chart. It provides a graphic illustration of price activity for the life of the futures contract being studied. Note the daily volume and open interest recorded at the bottom of the chart.

Chart courtesy of "Pocket Charts"

we are doing is highlighting some of the more common formations to give you an insight into how a trading system based on bar chart analysis might work.

The most common and significant formation is the trendline (Figure 3–3). It can be either an up or down trend line. Trendlines require at least two points to touch the line and are considered more reliable the closer they are to 45 degrees in incline or decline. A parallel line (dotted in Figure 3–3) is sometimes drawn to indicate a channel or trading range. Uptrend lines are drawn below the price ticks and downtrend above. The higher degree or steeper the trendlines are, the likelier they will be broken and the trend will reverse.

Figure 3–3: Up and Down Trendlines

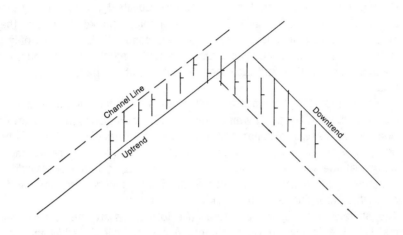

The most commonly used and, probably most watched chart formations, are simple up and down trendlines. The closer they are to 45 degrees, the more reliable they are believed to be.

All technical analysis is built on the premise that history repeats itself. When a trendline is established, technical traders expect it to continue. When it gets too steep, they expect the trendline to be broken. When a trendline is broken, they expect the trend to reverse. This mind set is part of what makes technical analysis work; what makes it a self-fulfilling prophecy.

Technical analysis also works because it is based on sound psychological principles, the most basic of which is herd psychology. When the trading herd sees a trendline, they trade it until it ends. When it ends, they look for the next trend or formation and trade it.

No one knows what the future will bring. It is a total unknown. Therefore, people (traders) who risk their money on anticipating where commodity prices will go next are uncertain, uncomfortable. When people are uneasy, they stick together. This basic need of man is responsible for history repeating itself and the meaningfulness of chart formation. As with anything else in life, none of the formations are anywhere near 100 percent reliable.

Support and resistance areas are very common and significant. There are places where downtrending markets come to rest repeatedly, or uptrending markets tend to stall repeatedly (Figure 3–4). For example, a market rallies and then falls back to a previous price level, from which a second rally is launched only to decline back to the same price level again. This is a support area. The opposite, where a market rallies time and again only to stall out at a certain price level, is a resistance area.

The reason for this phenomenon revolves around the fact the futures market is a zero-based market. For every winner, there is a loser. For every bull, a bear. For every long, a short. Areas of support and resistance are "zones of error." Thus, once a support area is penetrated, it becomes a resistance area because there are traders who bought at the support level and still hold their losing positions. They'd be happy at this point to get out at break even. These traders offset their losing positions, which props up the opposite side of the market.

Closely related to support and resistance formations are multiple tops and bottoms. Take the double top as an example. A market rallies, reaches an area of resistance, stalls, and begins to decline. After a short retracement, it rallies again,

Figure 3–4: Support and Resistance Levels

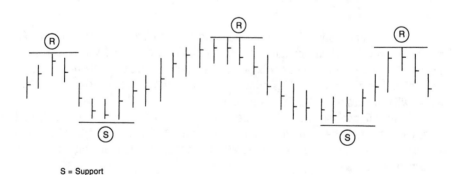

S = Support
R = Resistance

Commodity prices tend to find levels where traders believe the commodity is fairly priced or where prices appear to be too high. Downtrends stall or stop at support areas and uptrends stall or stop at resistance areas.

only to stall at the exact same resistance area. The chartist would call this a double top or "M" formation and consider it a sign of weakness. It would be a signal to short the market. The risk, of course, is that a triple top could develop. The trader who shorted the double top would be whipsawed by the market. Whipsawing is when you reverse your position only to have the market turn against you. You lose twice, once on your original position and again on your reversal. Multiple bottoms are the opposite of multiple tops.

More complex versions of the multiple tops or bottoms are the Head and Shoulders and Inverted Head and Shoulders formations. They resemble the silhouette of a person (Figure 3–5) and are very important for several reasons. First, they are considered very reliable by professional chartists. Furthermore, they foretell a major reversal in trend. Last of all, they can predict the length of the next move, or the reversal.

A head and shoulders formation usually consists of the following five key phases:

1. Left shoulder

2. Head

Figure 3–5: Head and Shoulder Formations

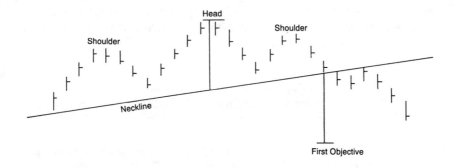

Professional chartists believe the Head and Shoulder and Inverted Head and Shoulder formations reliably foretell a major trend change. When they appear on a futures price chart, they bear watching.

3. Right shoulder

4. Neckline penetration

5. Prices often retrace and bounce off the neckline before heading toward their first price objective. This provides a second opportunity to short the market.

The first price objective is measured from the top of the head to the neckline and projected downward from the point where the neck was broken. A second, or even third, objective of the same distances can be projected, depending on the velocity of the market as it reaches the first objective. Inverted head and shoulders work just the opposite.

Another formation considered very reliable by chartists is the rounded bottom. These are long, drawn-out formations that can take months to mature. They are often called "saucer" bottoms because of their shape. When the saucer bottom matures, it signals a long term uptrend.

The reason for this is that while the rounded bottom is maturing, the price of the commodity is relatively low. It is at the bottom of its price range for a long time. While this occurs, it is not uncommon for new uses to develop that increase the long term demand. For example, while corn was making a rounded bottom in 1986-87, new uses for it, as gasohol and corn sweeteners, were developed. When it finally began a price rise, it had a stronger demand base and a long term bull move developed.

There are a lot of other bar chart patterns used by chartists, such as triangles, boxes, and key reversal days, but we can't cover them all. If you're serious about trading, you need to spend some time studying all the formations—so you'll at least know what other traders are likely to do.

Trend-Following Techniques

The second category we use to classify technical analysis techniques is trend-following. We'd like to quickly review two basic approaches. The first is moving averages.

These can be calculated for any period of time—three days, five, seven, 30, 200, whatever. Once calculated, they can be charted (Figure 3–6). To prepare the moving average, you can use the high, low, open or close. The latter is most

Figure 3–6: Price and Moving Average Chart

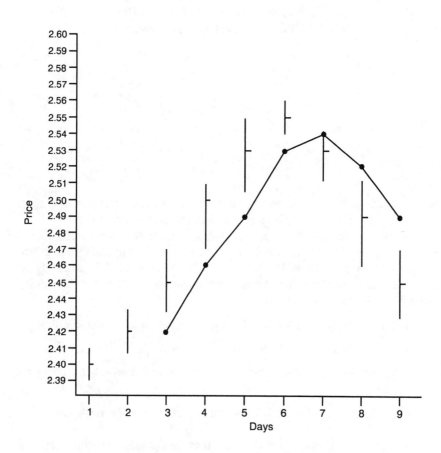

Note how this 3-day moving average lags the daily prices. Moving averages are used to smooth price action as a means of clarifying trends.

common. Naturally, you must consistently use the same one. Here's an example of how a three-day moving average is constructed:

Day #	Closing Price	Total of Last 3 Days	3-Day Average
1.	2.40		
2.	2.42		
3.	2.45	7.27	2.42
4.	2.50	7.37	2.46
5.	2.53	7.48	2.49
6.	2.55	7.58	2.53
7.	2.53	7.61	2.54
8.	2.49	7.57	2.52
9.	2.45	7.47	2.49

You can see that this procedure smoothes out the price volatility. The moving average lags the price activity both on the way up and the way down.

Some traders have developed trading systems from using combinations of moving averages. For example, you could use a set of moving averages of different lengths, a five and a 10-day. The slowest moving average, the 10-day in this case, gives the long term trend. The faster moving average, the five-day, provides the buy-sell signals. The rules are simple:

1. A buy signal occurs when the faster average crosses above the slower.

2. A sell signal occurs when it crosses below.

3. Offset long positions when daily price closes below either moving average.

4. Offset shorts when daily close is above either moving average.

The challenge is to uncover the set of moving averages that work best for the commodity(ies) you wish to trade.

Another sample of a mechanical trend-following system is the Point-and-Figure Chart. It is based on the theory that long periods of price consolidation are required to generate a significant price move. This system totally disregards time and concentrates solely on price movement.

Chartists use "X"s to denote upticks and "O"s for downticks. Therefore, much interday information is required and a scale must be set. Computer optimization programs are available to select scales. The only rule of thumb is that the scale must be larger than the minimum price fluctuation of the contract being charted. A popular scale is one cent value to each block with a three-cent reversal. This simply means that an X or an O is put on the chart for each one cent move up or down. Once three consecutive Xs or Os are recorded against the current trend, the trend is considered reversed, and positions are offset or reversed (Figure 3.7).

With this system, 45-degree angle trendlines and channels are considered to be even more significant than on bar charts. Other formations, like double bottoms and triangles, are also used in the analysis.

Figure 3–7: Point-and-Figure Chart

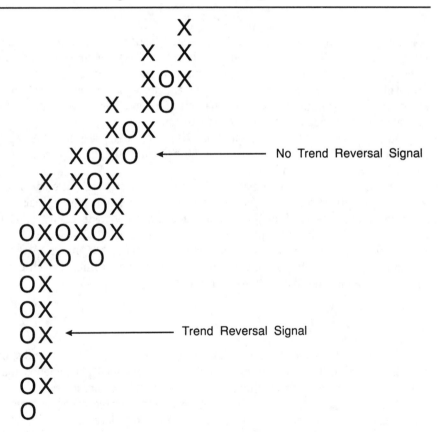

The "X"s denote positive price moves and the "O"s negative. These charts can be used as a mechanical trading system within themselves.

Structural Analysis

Technical analysts, who use this type of analysis, believe in the "Natural Law." The sun rises in the east each day. The seasons rotate from Spring, Summer, Fall, Winter. Patterns and respective cycles can be found everywhere. Physical sciences are based in this fact. Why not commodity prices? The structural analysts search for these patterns. Discussed below are a few of the more prominent schools of thought.

Seasonals

Seasonal patterns are the easiest to understand, especially if you consider the agricultural commodities. The seasonal price trends these commodities undergo reflect the regular annual changes that take place in their supply-demand equation.

Think about a typical crop year. First, we anticipate planting intentions. Then we worry and fret through the weather markets of the growing season. Finally, we usually have an abundance of supply at harvest time.

Studies have shown, for example, that 70 percent of all seasonal tops occur between April and July for soybeans, while 80 percent of the time soybean prices bottom between August and November.

How can you use this information? If you know the seasonal patterns for the commodity contracts you trade, you can use these patterns to confirm signals you get from other methods of analysis. Some traders will not trade against reliable seasonal patterns without having a very strong reason for doing so.

Seasonal patterns have been uncovered for virtually all futures markets. Learning the ones for the markets you trade is as basic as learning which chart formations are most reliable for those markets.

Cycles

Cycles are similar to seasonal patterns, but they can be longer than 12 months, or extremely short in duration. Cycles are built on the observed phenomenon that events have a tendency to repeat themselves at reasonably regular intervals.

As mentioned earlier, much of man's life is governed by repeatable patterns or cycles. Since man made and drives the commodity markets, it seems fair to assume that the markets would also possess definable cycles.

Cycles measure the time between each high or low (peaks and troughs). By knowing the time span between each high and low and the previous high and low, you are in a better position to anticipate the next high or low. Time is usually measured in calendar days, as opposed to trading days. Calendar days are used for the simple reason that people and nature do not take weekends off—money continues to change hands, as do events affecting cycles.

A long term cycle generally lasts a year or more; intermediate less than a year; short term ones last a few weeks or days. As a rule, allow approximately 10 percent leeway in the length of a cycle when establishing your expectation for the next top or bottom.

Elliott Wave

The Wave Principle states that social and market behavior trends and reverses in recognizable patterns. These patterns or waves reoccur. Prices unfold in "five waves" of crowd psychology when moving in the direction (up or down) of the primary trend. Then they move against the trend in "three waves." The wave pattern reflects life's starts, stops, false starts, and reversals. Progress is made in a jerky, sawtooth pattern, rather than a smooth up- or downtrend.

By isolating the exact position of the current price activity within the wave patterns allows the trader to profit by anticipating the market's next move. Once your trading becomes synchronized with the wave pattern, you can successfully ride the economic waves of the markets.

Gann Numbers

The best known of all structural analysts is probably W.D. Gann. His 1942 book, *How to Make Profits Trading Commodities,* was the first important treatise on this subject. He believed precise mathematical patterns govern everything, particularly the commodity markets. More importantly, he believed these patterns could be uncovered and exploited. Since his price predictions became legends in his own time and he claims to have made millions in the market, we can only assume he discovered many of them.

Integral to his trading system are Fibonacci Numbers—again a throwback to natural law—and angles of price trend movement. Together, his numbering system uncannily alerts traders to highs, lows, support-resistance areas, and reversal points. His work should be studied by every serious trader.

Again, this is not a definitive list of structural analytical systems. We just want, in this text, to give you an overview. Now we'll take a glance at character-of-market type systems.

Character-of-Market Analysis

We consider character-of-market analysis to be very sophisticated because it attempts to measure the quality of a price movement, and then take a position that may be opposite of the current trend. The other types of analysis discussed so far try to spot existing trends or certain formations that are reliable harbingers of future price activity.

With character-of-market analysis, the technician seeks what are known as "overbought" or "oversold" conditions. If the market is found to be overbought, it is sold. If it is found to be oversold, it is bought. This approach is a 180-degree turn from what we talked about with the trend-following approaches. With them, a strong market is bought and a weak one is sold.

The psychology behind character-of-market analysis is simply that when markets become too top heavy, they fall. Or when everyone gives up on prices ever rising again, they will. It is a contrarian approach to technical analysis. The trick is determining when a market is overbought or oversold. Here are some of the better known approaches.

Oscillators

Oscillators are concerned with price changes over a period of time. Simple oscillators use the difference between two moving averages. The departure between them indicates overbought and oversold conditions.

More complicated ones use the difference between daily prices. It can be the settlement, high-low, or opening price. Take a simple five-day settlement price oscillator as an example. It is computed by subtracting the settlement price of the fourth previous trading day from the current settlement price. If the settlement price has risen, you get a positive remainder. A negative remainder occurs if the price has fallen. If the remainder is exceptionally high or low, the analysts will consider the market overbought or oversold, and take the opposite position. Analysts using oscillators usually use more complicated ones than this simple example. But the basic concept is the same.

Williams' %R

An example of a more complex approach is the Williams' %R (©1979 by Larry R. Williams). For example, a five-day %R is computed as follows:

Subtract the settlement price of the latest trading day from the high price of the five-day period. Then divide that difference (i.e., the "change") by the difference (i.e., the "range") in the high price and the low price of the five-day period. Finally, multiply that result by 100. The range of %R is 0% to 100%.

According to Williams, when the value of %R enters the 90-100% range, the market is considered oversold. When the value enters the 0-10% range, the market is considered overbought.

Wilder's RSI

Another example of this intricate approach to the markets is the Relative Strength Index (Copyrighted 1978 by J. Wells Wilder, Jr.). It can best be described using the following formula:

$$RSI = 100 - (100/(1 + RS))$$

where RS = Up Avg/Dn Avg,
Up Avg = Up Sum/1
Dn Avg = DN Sum/L, and
L = number of days in RSI.

Again, this is a system that measures the change in price over a period of time to determine overbought-oversold situations.

Let's look at a 14-day RSI. To calculate RSI, the Up Sum is first computed by tabulating the positive changes in the settlement prices of successive trading days over the 15-day period, and adding those changes. The Dn Sum is computed by tabulating the negative changes in settlement prices over the period, and adding those changes. Then, Up Avg is computed by dividing Up Sum by 14; similarly for Dn Avg. Next Up Avg is divided by Dn Avg to get RS. And, finally, RSI is computed by adding 1 to RS, dividing this sum into 100, and subtracting that result from 100.

According to Wilder, when RSI exceeds 70, the market is considered overbought. When RSI is less than 30, the market is considered oversold.

When do you use character-of-market analysis?

This approach works best in choppy, zigzagging markets. If you use them in a long trending market, you may get burned badly. As we've said repeatedly, you need many tools on your technical analysis workbench. These are excellent ones to have when the market appears to be confused or erratic—but never rely on just one approach to analyzing all markets and all the varying market conditions.

Other Approaches

We can't spend a great deal of time on "other approaches" to technical analysis. There are simply too many of them, and most are too complex to be easily described. The best we can do is make you aware of a few of the possibilities.

Astrological Analysis—Astrology is the study of the aspects and positions of planets and other heavenly bodies to predict future human events. There are a number of books, and even a newsletter, devoted to commodity price analysis based on astrology. Lunar phases, planets—even sun spots—have also been used.

Correlation Analysis—This is the study of the relationship of a specific commodity to a related or non-related entity in the hopes that a correlation between the two (or more) will indicate future trends. A simple example is the correlation between gold and paper currencies, or gold and the U.S. budget deficit.

Fibonacci Numerical Progression Analysis—The classic name for this mathematical phenomenon is the golden ratio. It was originally recognized by the ancient Greek mathematicians and popularized in the 13th Century by Leonardo of Pisa, known as Fibonacci. The numerical series is created by starting with 1 and adding the results of each addition to the previous one—1, 2, 3, 5, 8, 13, 21, 34, 55, 89, (89 + 55 = 134) 134, etc. Using these numbers in various calculations as divisors or multipliers generate the golden ratio, which is 1.618 or 0.618. This ratio was called golden by the ancients because it appears widely in nature (branching of trees, flowers, sea shells, etc.) and is appealing to the eye. It was used in such varying structures as the Egyptian pyramids and the Sistine Chapel.

If it exists in nature, is used commonly by man and creates a pleasing design or formation. Technical analysts postulate that it should then appear in price charts as well. When it does, they give special emphasis to price advances or retracements that reflect the golden ratio. These technicians look for moves up or down of 62 percent or angles of this degree between critical points. No one is absolutely sure why this ratio is important, but in many cases it appears to work, and generates meaningful projections. W. D. Gann, as mentioned earlier, made extensive use of the golden ratio in his work.

Contrary Opinion

One last type of analysis you should be aware of is sometimes referred to as contrary opinion. It simply states that the masses are usually wrong. If the crowd or herd thinks a specific market is headed higher, it is probably ready to make a move lower.

The commodity markets are very fast moving, very emotional markets. Traders are called on to make split-second decisions, often involving large sums of money. Additionally, these decisions are not necessarily based in a cold, logical analysis of facts. Often, as you probably gathered from this discussion of fundamental and technical analysis, these decisions are more based in faith than anything else. This is only natural, since we're dealing in future events.

For this reason, you need to guard against being caught up in a stampede of bulls or bears. You must see when you've stopped following a trend, and have gotten caught up in a swell of emotion that keeps you in a market too long. Namely, beyond the point where it turns dramatically against you generating substantial losses. Contrary analysts believe that by the time the herd reacts, it is too late and things are about to change.

Combined Approaches

Using one type of analysis, even if one approach is technical and the other fundamental, does not preclude using others, even several others. The most common example is the analyst who uses a fundamental system to determine the long term trend and one or more technical systems for the short term.

We specifically said one or more technical systems for the short term because certain systems work better in certain types of markets and for certain commodities. For example, at times the commodity futures market in general, or a specific contract, has a tendency to trend up and down for long periods of time—three or four months or longer at a stretch. When this occurs, trend following systems (moving averages, etc.) work well.

But what happens when the markets get very choppy or trendless? Trend-following systems suffer severe whipsawing in non-trending markets. You probably want to use a character-of-the-market type of system in these very erratic types of markets.

Our point is that there is not a single trading approach that will be successful in all market conditions. If the activity of a market doesn't suit your system(s), you should change markets, or stand aside until more favorable conditions return.

Worksheet 3

1. True or false? Supply and demand are always in balance.

2. List 10 fundamental factors that could impact the price of the following commodities:

Live Hogs Precious Metals

Live Hogs	Precious Metals
A. _____	A. _____
B. _____	B. _____
C. _____	C. _____
D. _____	D. _____
E. _____	E. _____
F. _____	F. _____
G. _____	G. _____
H. _____	H. _____
I. _____	I. _____
J. _____	J. _____

3. Technical analysis is:

    A. A self-fulfilling prophecy.

    B. An analytical system relying solely on price and other statistical data.

    C. A system used by most professional traders.

4. True or False? Fundamental and technical analysis cannot be used together successfully.

5. What are the types of technical analysis and give an example.

Types	Example
A. _____	_____
B. _____	_____
C. _____	_____
D. _____	_____

E. _____   _____

6. What is the best, most successful trading approach?

   A. Fundamental

   B. Technical

   C. Combination of Fundamental and Technical

   D. None of the above

Answers to Worksheet 3

1. The answer is false. When supply and demand are in balance, price moves sideways. This rarely happens for any extended period of time.

2. Ten fundamental factors that could impact the price of the following commodities are:

Live Hogs	Precious Metals
A. Weather	A. Federal government policies
B. Consumer preferences	B. Politics
C. Hog numbers	C. Mining activity
D. Farrowings	D. Balance of trade figures
E. Corn prices	E. Business cycle
F. Interest rates	F. Industrial usage
G. Slaughter rates	G. Use in coinage and jewelry
H. Competitive meat prices	H. Consumer attitudes
I. Disposable income	I. World economy
J. Gross farm income	J. Currency exchange rates

It's impossible to list all the possible fundamental factors that can influence the price of a commodity. Not to mention the variations possible. On top of this, the fundamental analyst has to qualify and, more critically, quantify each factor. For these reasons, most professional traders have opted to use technical analysis.

3. All of these are correct.

4. This statement is false. It is not uncommon for a trader to use fundamental analysis to determine the long-term trend and technical for the mid to short term.

5. The five basic classifications of technical analysis are:

Types	Example
A. Price Bar Chart Analysis	Formation Recognition and Analysis
B. Trend Following	Moving Averages, Point and Figure
C. Structural	Seasonals, Cycles, Waves
D. Character-of-Market	Williams' %R, Wilder's RSI
E. Other	Moon Cycles, Sun Spots

6. There is no right or wrong answer to the question of what is the best trading system. You must decide for yourself what works for you. Most of the successful traders we know have a system that is composed of many varied elements.

4

Placing Orders in the Markets Correctly

Key Concepts

◆ Types and uses for the various orders needed to place trades in the commodity markets.

◆ Elements of a properly executable commodity order.

◆ How orders are executed in the trading "pits."

◆ Checking on a "bad fill."

You place orders with your broker. Normally this is done by phone. Occasionally you may visit your broker's office and trade in person. We recommend, if it is physically practical, that you visit your broker's office at least once to get a better feel for how their system works. On the other hand, with all the electronic communication equipment available—phones, telephone conferencing, facsimile machines, cable, TV, computer modems, and satellite dishes—personal visits aren't as important as they used to be. We have seen innumerable cases of successful customer-broker relationships where there have never been any face-to-face meetings.

To properly place orders, you need to fully understand the alternatives available to you. The following provides an overview of the more common types of orders.

Market Orders

When you are considering placing an order, the first thing you need to consider is whether you wish to place any price, time, or other restrictions on it. If you don't, and wish to get in or out of a market (position) as quickly as possible, you use a market order. This is also the most common type of order.

"Buy me one COMEX December silver at the market."

This tells your broker which side (long or short) of the market you wish to be on, the number of contracts, exchange, and delivery month.

Also, it tells your broker you want to be filled immediately. You want to buy at the going price—no matter what that price is. You wish to get in or out (this could be an offsetting position) of a market without any restrictions on the price you get filled at.

The risk you take is twofold. First, you could get a "bad fill." This is one that occurs at the fringe of the trading range, usually during low volume days. For example, you called your broker with the above order. Silver traded that day between $5.50 and $5.55. You get filled at $5.55 or the high of the day. With a little luck or better timing, you could have been filled at the low or somewhere in between. Since each $0.01 change in silver equals $50.00, a fill that was two or three cents better could mean an additional profit of $100.00 or $150.00.

Secondly, market orders take top priority in the trading pits. They are the first orders to be filled, since there are no restrictions on them. In fast-moving markets, your orders could be filled within minutes of the time you talked with your broker. Once in the market, you have no guarantee it will move in your favor. This means you could begin losing money within seconds of hanging up from placing an order. On the other hand, you could be making money just as quickly.

Our point is simple—market orders get you in the market fast. Use them when you want to make a quick entry or exit.

The alternatives to a market order are orders with time, price, or other restrictions. When you put conditions on an order, you risk not having the order executed (filled). This could be costly. You could be in a market that is moving against your position. With each tick of the quotation equipment, you're losing money. This is the time to use a market order—forget the restrictions. Get out as fast as you can.

Market on Open

Time restrictions mean the floor broker must execute the order during a specified period of time. Market on Open Orders (MOO) are an example. These orders are traded, at the beginning of a trading session. Most exchanges designate the first 15 minutes as the "opening." An opening trading range is established and you are entitled to a fill within this range if there is sufficient trading volume.

If for some reason, your order cannot be executed during the opening period, it is automatically cancelled. You receive an "unable." If you decide you still wish to make a trade during that trading session, you must reenter your order.

Market on Close

Market on Close (MOC) is the same as Market on Open, only it is designated to be traded during the last five minutes of a trading session. Again, if for some reason your order cannot be filled, you would be notified. Additionally, since MOC orders are for the closing period, you don't get a second change to reenter the order in that trading session. If you still need the position, you must wait for the next trading session.

MOO and MOC orders become market orders during the opening or closing periods respectively. This means they get top priority from the floor brokers and are normally filled without any problems. The only hang-up would be extremely low volume days or days when the market is locked limit up or down and no, or very limited, trading occurs. The only restriction on the price is that it is within the opening or closing range.

Day, GTC, GT Orders

Besides these two time-limit types of orders, you can also place day trade orders, good until cancelled (GTC) orders, and good through (GT) orders. Day orders are limited to execution the same day, or to a single trading session. At the end of the trading session, the order is cancelled if it hasn't been filled. If there are two trading sessions of the commodity being traded, your day order would not carry over to the evening session on most exchanges. The exchanges set the trading rules and they can vary between exchanges. These rules are then reviewed and approved by the CFTC (Commodity Futures Trading Commission).

Don't confuse a day order with day trading. A day trade is opened and offset during a single trading session. You designate a day trade when you place it because you often get a lower commission for two reasons. First you, your broker and his/her firm do not have the risk of something going wrong with your trade overnight. Day trading is considered a little less risky because it is short term. Just think about the risk of holding a position in crude oil overnight, when Iraq invaded Kuwait. If you are day trading and some unexpected news hits the trading pits, you can react. If something occurs when you and you broker are asleep, you may awake to a market that opens limit up or down against your position(s).

The second reason for a lower brokerage commission rate on day trading is volume. Day traders usually trade more often because of the short term nature of their trading system. They are completing several trades each trading day. Position traders, on the other hand, hold trades for days, weeks, and months.

The next limit type order to be aware of is the good until cancelled or "good till cancelled" (GTC) order. With this type of order, it stays in the market until filled. Most exchanges will not accept GTC orders, but you can have the order desk of the brokerage firm put your order in each day until you get a fill.

Variations of the GTC are the "good through the week" (GTW), "good through month" (GTM), and "good through" a specific time during a trading session. The financial danger is losing track of these types of orders and getting fills long after the price trend has changed or long after you want the trade. For this reason, we don't usually recommend them.

Price Limit Orders

Besides time limit orders, you can use price limit orders. These are orders that put restrictions on the price the floor broker can bid or accept on your behalf. These are different from market orders that, as you remember, the floor broker can buy or sell at any price.

The simplest of these is the limit order. You use it when you wish to specify a certain price level. For example, a buy limit order can only be filled at the limit price or a price below it (a better price). If you place a limit price order to buy (go long) silver at $5.00 an ounce, your fill will be at least $5.00, or less than $5.00.

On a sell (short) limit order, the floor broker must fill your order at your limit price or above it. These are sometimes called "Or Better" orders. They must get filled at your price or better.

Now this sounds great, but there are a few hitches. First, any order with any type of restriction takes a lower priority than a market order. Secondly, the conditions (limits) you put on your order may prevent it from being filled. On the silver $5.00 limit buy order just mentioned, what happens if silver never trades at $5.00 or lower? Silver could move down to $5.01 and then shoot up to $6.00 or a $0.99 profit (5,000 X $0.99 = $4,950.00) and you would have missed the move. With a market order, you would have enjoyed the move. This is the chance you take with limit orders.

Why do traders put any kind of limit on their orders? The most common answer is that they want certain technical criteria to be met to satisfy their trading system before they place a trade. If their conditions are not met, these traders would rather stand aside the market. For example, it's common for a trader to want uptrend lines or a support area to be penetrated before going short a market.

Stop Orders

A variation of the limit order is the stop order. The stop price is the limit, but when the stop price is reached, the order becomes a market order. In other words, a sell stop becomes a market order only when the commodity trades at or below—or is offered in the pits at or below—the stop price. On the other side of the market, a buy stop order becomes a market order when the trading is at or above the stop price.

Traders use stop orders to control or manage losses. If they are long, you place a sell stop below a resistance area, for example. This is designed to get you out of losing positions if they begin to move against you. If you were short, you would use a buy stop as a protective stop.

Some trading systems use stop orders to reverse positions. These are systems that are always trading in a particular market. Let's say a system is long five oat contracts, which is a market that often trends up or down for reasonably long periods of time. As the oats' contract moves up, a trading reversal stop order—which will sell or short 10 oat futures contracts—is placed just below appropriate support levels, perhaps a long term trendline. This stop order calls for twice as many contracts as the trader has in the market. This way, when the stop is hit, the trader switches to the short side with five contracts—thus the long position is offset and a new short position is established. This is known as a reversal stop because it completely reverses the original position.

With all grains, keep in mind when placing orders that the quantity represents the number of 1,000-bushel units. To buy one corn, oat, wheat, or soybean contract on the Chicago Board of Trade (CBOT), you place an order for five corn, oats, wheat or soybeans. The actual stop-reversal order in the above paragraph would be to sell 50 oats, in order to be net short five contracts once the long position is offset.

You can combine the stop order with limit restriction. With the stop-limit order, the order is triggered when the stop price is hit, but must be filled at, or at a better price than the limit.

There are also a few orders, other than time and price limitation orders, that you should become familiar with. One is the "fill or kill" (FOK) order. This instructs your broker that if your order cannot be filled immediately, it should be cancelled. This order is often used in highly volatile or very slow moving markets. You either want to get a position quickly, or you want to stand aside.

"Give Ups"

Let's say you're traveling, or on vacation, and something happens in the market. You want to make a trade, but before you do you need to look at a chart, or review some technical data. You go to a local brokerage office of a firm different from the one at which you have an account. If this firm is cooperative, they'll share with you the information you need and offer to place an order as a "give up" to your firm. They may ask for some identification and proof you have an active account. Most of the time, it is just easier to call your own broker to place an order. But this is an option you may occasionally need and should be aware exists.

There are other commands or order clarifications you should know. For example, when placing combination orders, like "spreads" or "straddles," there are two reasons you should state these when you place your order with your broker. First, it alerts your broker to what's coming, so he/she can check to make sure both legs are correct. Second, these types of combination trades sometimes have a lower commission rate than if each of the legs of the spread was placed separately.

Spread trades can be entered as market or limit orders. When you use a limit order, you specify the amount of premium (or spread) one leg is to have over the other. Also, it is customary to state the buy side first.

You should also alert your broker when you are switching or rolling over a position. You do this when you want to stay in a position—let's say long copper—but the contract month you are in is about to go into delivery. You then close out your position in the expiring month, and reestablish it in another delivery month that has time left in it. Some traders like to stay in the spot month (the one that's about to expire) for three reasons. First, it usually has the most liquidity. Secondly, the spot month in some commodities doesn't have limits. And, third, it is the contract that most resembles the cash markets.

Discretionary (DRT) Orders

There are various degrees of discretion you can give your broker. The maximum is when you execute a Limited Power of Attorney and let your broker trade your account with total discretion. What is more common is to give a broker a little discretion in order to get an order filled. This can be done without signing over power of attorney. To do this, you must make all the other decisions about the trade, namely commodity (including delivery month), side (long or short), and quantity (number of contracts).

Let's say you want to get into a nervous market, in which prices are bouncing up and down. Nevertheless, you are confident it is about to make a move higher. You tell your broker to go long at a certain price, but he can be plus or minus a certain range of points or cents. Be sure to restrict your broker to a range, don't give him *carte blanche* on price.

Another example is "time" discretion. You and your broker get together one evening and decide to make a certain trade—if the market opens higher the next day. You will be out of touch during the opening. You give your broker the discretion to place the order after the opening, if the conditions agreed upon are reached.

This is by no means an exhaustive discussion of orders. It covers the most common ones you need on a day-to-day basis. There are more sophisticated ones you'll learn to use as you gain experience.

An additional aspect to consider regarding orders is that each exchange has rules regarding the types of orders they accept. For example, the Chicago Board of Trade doesn't accept open orders. Also, there are differences between some of the pits on an exchange. COMEX, for example, accepts open orders in all the pits except gold. The table below provides some additional examples.

Exchanges

Type Orders	CBT	CME (IMM)	MIDAM	COMEX	NYME
Market	Yes	Yes	Yes	Yes	Yes
Open	No	Yes	Yes	Yes (Except gold)	Yes
Market on Close (MOC)	Yes	Yes	Yes	Yes	Yes
Stop	Yes	Yes	Yes	Yes	Yes
Market if touched (MIT)	No	Yes	Yes (In corn, hogs, and cattle)	Yes	No

This table is only a sampling of the exchange rules, which will change over time. Therefore, once you know which orders suit your trading or your system of entering and exiting markets, and which futures contracts and exchanges you'll be trading, you can check with your broker to verify that the exchange you'll be trading through allows you to use the orders you want in the pit(s) you plan to trade.

When your broker (or his/her order desk) calls an order into the order desk on the floor of the exchange, it is done in this fashion:

1. Your trading account number

2. The side of the trade you want to be on—long, short, both (spread, straddle).

3. The quantity of contracts in the transaction.

4. Delivery month and year (if necessary).

5. The contract to be traded.

6. Type of order.

It would sound something like this: "For account number 123456, buy me five June silver MOC." This would get you long five silver contracts in the June contract during the last five minutes of trading of the current trading session. The exchange called would determine the size of the contract, namely 5,000 troy ounces on COMEX or 1,000 troy ounces on the MIDAM. If an exchange had two different size contracts, a mini or a maxi in the same market, this would be specified.

Your task is to communicate to your broker what you want to do. The broker's job is to get it placed correctly in the market.

Placing orders is one area you need to consider when selecting a broker. If you decide to open an account with a discount broker, you'll be expected to call your orders into a clerk at an order desk. You don't necessarily talk to the same clerk each time—nor is the clerk familiar with your strategy, system, or current positions. This clerk has no way of second-guessing your order for errors. In other words, it's not the clerk's place to double check what you tell him.

For example, let's say you are long five soybean contracts. You're ready to offset them and take profits. You call the order desk and tell them to go short five beans at the market. Are you now offset? What does the clerk do? The clerk calls the floor and offsets one of your bean positions, since grains are traded in per thousands of bushel lots. You are still long four contracts. The correct order, to offset all your long positions, would have been to go short 25 soybeans.

An order clerk at a discount brokerage probably would not question you whether you wanted to offset one or all of your positions. At a full service brokerage firm, you would expect your broker to ask. Your broker would have worked with you before you put the positions on, updated you as the market progressed, and would know what your objectives are.

For these and other reasons, we recommend using full service brokerage firms, at least until you become experienced in this phase of the business. Mistakes can become very expensive fast. In our soybean example, the trader would have been long four soybean contracts in a declining market—that's 20,000 bushels of soybeans. If the market drops just a nickel per bushel before the trader realizes he placed the order incorrectly, it would be a $1,000.00 error. And, it could get a whole lot worse, if left unchecked.

"A Game of Inches!"

Occasionally, you may place an order and get back what is called a "bad fill" or an unexpected "unable." A bad fill is simply a fill at a price that is worse than you expected. It usually is a price on the wrong end of the day's trading range. For example, you place a sell order and received a fill at the very bottom of an eight-cent price range. If your fill had been in the middle of the range or at the price when you put the order into the market, you would have had a $0.04 profit for the day. Four cents worth of silver or soybeans would be $200.00, not a bad start to a trade. If you had gotten a "good fill," you might have picked up $0.05, $0.06, or even $0.07 of the move. Another possibility occurs when you place an order you think is in the trading range, yet it isn't filled. The order comes back "unable" to fill.

If you or your broker think you have not been fairly treated by the floor, there is a way to check an order. You can request a "Time and Sale Report" (Figure 4–1).

To understand what's behind a Time and Sale Report, let's quickly review how prices are reported from the trading pits. To begin, the trading floors of all the major exchanges are divided into trading pits or rings. They get the term pit or ring from the physical layout of the trading area. It has various levels of steps on which the floor traders stand so they can easily see and hear each other. Many of the "market markers" for each specific contract are in the center of the pits. The pits are circular or octagonal in shape, therefore the term "rings."

The actual trading is done by open outcry. This simply means the brokers call out their orders so anyone (who is a member of that particular exchange) in the pit can hear them. Because of the high noise level, a system of hand signals has also been devised to supplement the open outcry.

The exchanges employ market reporters to record price changes as they occur. These people are next to or in the pits, depending on the exchange. The prices are displayed on "electronic chalkboards" (the board in "Board of Trade") above the trading floor. Nowadays, electronic (closed-circuit television) quotation screens may also be in the pits. The market reporters communicate with the exchange's communications center via portable radios. Computer operators, in the "com" center, input the prices into their computer for editing and dispersal to the world via satellite uplinks and other electronic means. The days of the actual ticker tape are long gone.

Now, this is a key point—the market reporters report what they see (hand signals) and hear (open outcry). They don't always know if a bid or ask price has been accepted. When the trading level permits, the bid or ask price is designated as such. At times, the market moves too fast to permit separating bids and asks. In

Figure 4–1: Time and Sale Report

Time	Price	Time	Price
10:08:54	37120	10:10:28	37140
08:56	10	10:32	50
09:00	15	10:42	60
09:00	20	10:40	50
09:02	25	10:40	45
09:11	20	10:42	40
09:16	25	11:02	30
09:23	20	11:02	25
09:26	25	11:19	20
09:26	30	11:19	30
09:42	35*	11:19	35
09:49	30	11:31	40
09:49	35	11:31	45
09:49	40	11:41	40
09:51	50	11:48	40
10:09:56	37145	10:11:59	37145

very fast moving markets, you may not be able to distinguish bids, asks, and sales. But in these markets, it usually doesn't matter because fills are usually immediate.

We call your attention to this because you may have some experience with the security exchanges. In the security market, the price reporting system only carries actual transactions. This is not the case in the futures market. Occasionally, this difference may be reflected in your fill. You may be placing an order based on what you think is the last transaction, only to learn it was a bid or ask that was never filled.

This brings us back to the Time and Sale Report. You can request one from the floor. It will be sent to your broker via facsimile machine as quickly as the order clerk on the floor can run one off. Much depends on the level of activity when you request one. We have received them back in less than an hour. Other times, it has taken longer.

The report shows you the transactions that took place before and after the time you placed your order. Note the asterisk on Figure 4.1 at 10:09:42, which was when the order being checked was received at the floor. The purpose of the report is to explain why you got the price you did, or why it was impossible to fill your order. If you still feel you deserve a fill, your broker can talk to the pit or floor supervisor. You may be accommodated, depending on the rules of the specific exchange.

To get a Time and Sales Report, all you do is request it from your broker. He or his order desk supervisor calls the exchange and requests an "order check," giving the floor order number of the order to be checked. As soon as possible, the Time and Sales Report is faxed to your broker. You and your broker review it and decide what to do.

To thoroughly understand the "price discovery" process—that is one of the main functions of all exchanges—you must visit an exchange on a busy day. These are open markets; open to all members of the exchange. The orders must be placed so that any member of the exchange can fill them. Thus the use of open outcry.

Equally important to understand is the enormous volume of business that is conducted, not to mention the velocity at which it takes place. For example, the number of futures contracts per month traded at U.S. exchanges usually exceeds 20,000,000—that annualizes to over 250,000,000 or a quarter of a billion. Additionally, you must keep in mind that various contract months are being traded in different parts of a pit. This means minor discrepancies can emerge from the frenzy of trading. These unexpected misalignments, especially when they hurt your position, can make you feel as if you've been treated unfairly. If you can arrange to spend a day or a few hours on the floor of a major exchange, you will get a feel for the challenge it is to keep all the prices flowing in an orderly fashion.

The regulations of the Chicago Board of Trade explain it like this—"whenever price fluctuations of the commodities dealt in on the exchange are rapid and the volume of business is large, it is a common occurrence that different prices are bid and offered for the same delivery month in different parts of the pit at the same time. The normal result of such conditions is, at times, the execution by members of orders at prices not officially quoted or the inability of a member to execute an order at a limited price. This is unavoidable, but is not the fault of anyone. Members may not readjust the price at which orders have been filled or report as filled orders that have not been filled." Now, members cannot make adjustments, but exchange officials occasionally do. For example, the closing range is sometimes adjusted after the market closes on very hectic days. This is done only to more accurately reflect what occurred in the pits.

Other errors or changes can occur that impact your orders or your account. For example, the exchanges can change margins unexpectedly. Margin changes happen hundreds of times each year as the exchanges adjust to changing conditions. An unexpected margin adjustment can put your account in debit. Your futures commission merchant (FCM) might demand more equity be added to your account or they'll "blow you out of the market." They have a right to do this, given to them in the account papers you signed.

Our point is simply this—be prepared for the unexpected. Sometimes it will be to your favor, other times it will cost you money. When it happens, don't panic. Talk to your broker. Learn your rights. Act judiciously.

Summary

The key elements of a futures order, as you give it to your broker, are as follows:

1. Side—long, short, spread, etc.

2. Number of contracts.

3. Exchange, if there could be any confusion as to which one.

4. Delivery month, year (if there are delivery months overlapping 2 years).

5. Futures contract.

6. Type of order.

Here are some examples of various types of orders.

Market Order
"Buy one COMEX March silver at the market."

Market on Open or Close
"Sell five January soybeans MOC."

Day Trade
"Buy three May soybean oil at the market Day Trade."

Good Through
"Sell 10 March CBOT wheats at $2.75 or better GTC."

Price Limit
"Buy seven April Live Cattle at 59.65 or better."

Stop Orders
"Sell six Feb Pork Bellies 62.10 stop."

Fill or Kill
"Buy four September coppers at 99 cents Kill or Fill"

Spread
"Spread Buy eight March Cocoa Sell eight December Cocoa Even."

Rollover
"Roll Buy three March Crude Oil Sell three December Crude Oil."

Discretionary
"Buy one March World Sugar 9.00 two points discretion."

You won't have to use this exact terminology with your broker, nor is this a definitive discussion of all the possible orders you can use. For example, there are orders to instruct your broker to scale up or down your position, or to re-tender an unwanted delivery.

The purpose of this discussion is to give you an insight into the wide variety of possible orders that can be used. You are not limited to straight market orders, as some believe. What you need to do is discuss with your broker in as much detail as necessary, what you wish to accomplish with your order. Then work together to decide the type of order to use.

Worksheet 4: Placing Orders

1. List the information you (or your broker) needs to place an order in the futures market.

   A. _____

   B. _____

   C. _____

   D. _____

E. _____

F. _____

G. _____

2. True or False? Chicago Board of Trade rules state you cannot question a fill.

3. Match the columns

A. Market Orders	Same as price limit order
B. Limit Orders	Discretionary abbreviation
C. Stop Limit	Standing order until filled
D. MOO	Filled immediately or cancel
E. MOC	When limit price hit becomes market order
F. Day	Broker allowed to decide when to enter order
G. GTC	Filled during last five minutes of trading
H. GT	Must be filled at limit price or better
I. Or Better	Top priority order
J. FOK	Good only during trading session
K. DRT	Good through (specify time period)
L. Time Discretion	Fill during first 15 minutes of trading

4. Write an order to sell five July corn contracts at a price of not more than $2.55 per bushel.

   _____

5. If you opened a position on both sides (long and short) of related markets, you would be _____.

6. True or False? When you give your broker discretion, he has the right to trade your account any way he sees fit.

7. True or False? You can place any type of order you wish in any exchange.

8. True or False? When you place a market order, you are guaranteed a fill.

9. True or False? Every order called into an exchange is filled in an orderly fashion.

10. Floor brokers handle orders depending on their priority. Rate the priority of the following types of orders. One being the highest and three the lowest.

    Price Limit _____

    Kill or Fill _____

    Market _____

Answers to Worksheet 4

---

1. The following is needed to place an order in the futures market.

   A. The account number.

   B. To buy or sell or spread.

   C. Number of contracts.

   D. Month of delivery and, if necessary, exchange.

   E. Year, if necessary, when there are contract months extending into the next calendar year.

   F. The futures contract to be traded.

   G. The type of order (restrictions, if any), Market, Limit, OCO, MOO, MIT, Stop-Limit, MIT, etc.

2. The answer is false. You always have a right to question the fills you receive and, if you think it is necessary, you can request a Time & Sales Report.

3. Answers to matching columns.

   I. Same as Price Limit Order

   K. Discretionary abbreviation

   G. Standing order until filled

   J. Filled immediately or cancel

   B. When limit price hit, it becomes a market order

L. Broker allowed to decide when to enter order

E. Filled during last five minutes of trading

C. Must be filled at limit price or better

A. Top priority order

F. Good only during trading session

H. Good through (specify time period)

D. Fill during first 15 minutes of trading

4. "Sell 25 July corn at 2.55 or better."

5. Spreading—The simultaneous buying and selling of two related markets in the expectation that a profit will be made when the positions are offset.

6. The answer is false. There are various levels of discretion. You can verbally give your broker very limited discretion regarding the time or an acceptable price range for a specific order. Or, you can give written (limited power of attorney) discretion to your broker to do all the trading for you. But even if you do sign a Limited Power of Attorney, the broker must trade your account within guidelines established by federal regulators, as well as his/her supervisors.

7. False. Each exchange establishes its own set of rules that are approved by the Commodity Futures Trading Commission (CFTC). Part of this set of rules states the type of orders that can be used on its trading floor(s). This may even vary from one trading pit to another. Therefore, you must rely on your broker to counsel you regarding the type of acceptable orders on each exchange or trading ring.

8. This is not necessarily true. Most of the markets have daily trading limits. These are the maximum price ranges (up or down) specific futures contracts can trade in a single trading session. If the price is bid above or below these limits, no trading takes place. These are called "limit up" or "limit down" days. When this occurs, even market orders are returned "unable."

9. This is a trick question designed to get you to think about how the system works.

Orders enter and exit the markets in a very orderly fashion. You call your broker. Your broker or his/her order desk calls the order clerk at the exchange. Your order is given to a floor broker. Once filled, the order moves back up the chain. The floor clerk calls your broker with your fill. Your broker notifies you.

Chaos reigns in the middle of this process. Once the floor broker receives your order, he/she attempts to fill it. This is done through the system of "open outcry," combined with hand signals. In an active pit, different contract months may be traded in different parts. All the brokers, as many as 100 or more, are calling out and flashing orders—filling thousands of orders an hour. This explains why you can occasionally receive a fill that seems out of line. But you can always check it out by requesting a Time and Sales Report.

10. Speed is of the utmost when trading futures. The more restrictions on an order, the lower priority the floor broker will give it. Since market orders have no restrictions, they get the highest priority. Kill or fill orders must be executed right away or canceled. Therefore, they get second priority. Limit orders are third because the limit price must be reached or exceeded to allow the floor broker to fill it.

5

Search for the Holy Grail or How to Find or Develop the Perfect Trading System

---
Key Concepts

◆ Putting the Law of Probability to work in your commodity trading.

◆ The three rights—time, side, commodity.

◆ Developing your personal commodity trading system.

◆ Picking winners!

◆ Learning from and about the Wasendorf Trading System.

Just as the Knights of the Round Table never found the Holy Grail, the odds are you will not come up with the perfect trading system. But this doesn't mean you cannot develop a successful approach to trading.

Success in futures trading means making more money than you lose. This is no easy task since the vast majority of traders are net losers. Even many of the great traders—take Richard Dennis—have disastrous periods.

The key phrase is "making more money than you lose." Losing money is a given. You must be prepared psychologically and financially to deal with this eventuality.

Another way of looking at this reality is the Law of Probability. Experienced traders know that to be net winners, they must spread their trading equity over as many markets as reasonable and/or trade as many times as possible. For example, if your trading system provides signals in several markets, the odds of you always picking the single, best market opportunity of the many potential ones is remote.

Let's say your system tracks ten distinct commodity markets. It gives you a buy signal in five of them on a given day. What do you do? Do you trade all five? Do you trade only the one with the strongest signal? Do you look to other analytical tools for confirmation?

What you do depends on your system. What you don't do refers back to the Law of Probability. It tells experienced traders they cannot expect to pick winners every time. To be successful, they must spread their trading equity over several market opportunities. It's not uncommon for professional traders to trade one or two opportunities in each of the major commodity categories—grains, meats, metals, financials, and food/fiber. They know that on any given trading day, or over any given period of time, not all the commodities are making moves up or down. The excitement in the pits seems to move from one to another, rarely are they all moving at once.

The Three Rights

To make money, you must be in the right market, on the right side of the market, and at the right time. You are investing in what you expect to happen in the future—five minutes, five days, or five months from the moment you call your broker and place your order. You have no way of knowing if you will be right or wrong until afterwards.

At the same time, you must protect your risk capital as carefully as possible. This requires sound money management techniques, which is the second part of the Law of Probability. A sure way of ending a trading career abruptly is putting all your risk capital on one or two trades. A "double or nothing" approach to the markets will invariably, in our opinion, lead to you ending up with nothing.

Just as you increase the probability of being in the right market at the right time on the right side by trading several different markets, you'll increase your probability of success by putting no more than 10 percent of your risk capital on any one trade. This gives you at least ten opportunities to select one or more trades to pay for the ones that lose or just break even.

You must further consider what is known as the "distribution of winning-losing trades." For example, your distribution might look like this:

Trade Distribution:
    10 trades executed
    5 winners
    5 losers

Of the five winners:
    3 small or break even
    1 modest size
    1 big or decent size

Of the five losers:
    4 small
    1 modest

Your objective is to let winners run and cut losers shorts. If you do an analysis of the trading performance of the most successful CTAs (professional commodity trading advisers), you rarely find a winning percentage higher than 60 percent.

Keep in mind, the prime objective is to make money, not to generate a high percentage of profitable trades. You can be a net winner with a low percentage of winning trades. By low, we mean 40 percent, 30 percent or even 20 percent.

To do this, you must be very disciplined. You develop, for example, strict rules for exiting losing trades. When a trade begins to make money, you place a trailing stop behind it (below a long position or above a short). Eventually this stop position is taken out, offsetting your position. In other words, the market decides for you when to close a position.

Your Personal Trading System

From all we have said so far, you should be coming to the conclusion there are many facets to a trading system. You must do research using fundamental and/or technical analysis, select specific trades and markets, and follow your trad-ing/money management rules. All these functions blend, and are inseparable.

Let's review some of the characteristics of a good trading system. First of all, it suits your personality. If you are not a detail-oriented person, a system that requires constant tending, adjustments, and information will not fit your needs.

You must also take into account your tolerance for risk. Some systems, like people, are more conservative than others. Another critical aspect is complexity. A system can be as simple as two or three rules governing the behavior of two moving averages to a computerized econometric model. By the way, there is a plethora of trading systems written for personal computers on the market today. If you have a computer, you should take a serious look at them. We'll return to the subject of futures trading and computers in a later chapter.

Selecting Trades

How do you decide which commodity within a complex to trade? Why corn and not oats? Or why silver and not gold or copper? The best way of answering this question may be to describe how a trading system works. Since we know the most about our own, and since it has been up and running for over a decade, we'll use it as our example. Please keep in mind, we're not recommending it for you—just using it as an example.

The Wasendorf Trading System

The origin of this system resides in the work of Charles Dow. In his observations on the stock market, he came to the conclusion that it is very difficult to determine the overall trend of the market by studying individual stock issues. Therefore, he began to average them, which eventually became known as the Dow Jones Aver-ages. He further refined this approach by creating sub-groups, such as the industri-als and railroads (now transportation). By comparing the sub-group averages to the overall average, you can determine which sub-group is "moving the market"—the leaders and/or laggers.

We, at Wasendorf, first attempted to use one of the many existing indexes while we were developing Index Analysis as a unique technical analysis tool. Unfortunately, we could not find one suited for the purpose. The primary draw-back, in our opinion, of the indexes we studied, was that they were not responsive enough to market changes to be tradeable. Therefore, we developed a proprietary index, the Wasendorf Composite Index (WCI). To make it responsive, we incorporated open interest of all the contract months being traded in each commodity used in the formula. Additionally, we incorporated the price of the spot month because it most resembles the cash market, usually has the most volatility, and in many markets has no daily price limit. These unique features, in our opinion, give this index the market simulation needed to allow the meaningful use of traditional technical approaches to analysis. Taking another page out of Charles Dow's book, we divided the WCI into four sub-indexes. See Figure 5–1 for a breakdown of commodities, Figure 5–2 for an illustration of it.

It is important to note that gold is not a part of the index. It was left out so we could compare the indexes to the price of gold, which we consider as an index of world inflation. The financials and currencies were also omitted. Again, these markets perform like indexes themselves. For example, currencies and interest rates, in our opinion, reflect the buying power and financial conditions of the countries they represent. We like to compare the physical commodity markets, as

Figure 5–1: Breakdown of Wasendorf Composite Index by Its Sub-Indexes

Grains Sub-Index

Corn, Soybeans, Soybean Meal, Soybean Oil, Chicago Wheat, Minneapolis Wheat, Kansas City Wheat, and Oats

Meats Sub-Index

Live Hogs, Live Cattle, Pork Bellies, and Feeder Cattle

Metals Sub-Index

Silver, Platinum and Copper

Food & Fiber Sub-Index

Cocoa, Coffee, Sugar, Lumber, Cotton and Orange Juice

Figure 5-2: Long Term Wasendorf Composite Index and Its Four Sub-Indexes

These indexes provide an insight into the price movement of the primary physical commodity markets. It is divided into four sub-indexes—grains, meats, metals and food/fiber.

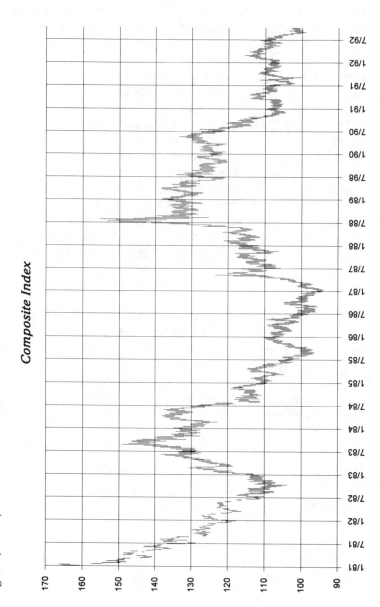

Composite Index

Grains Sub-Index

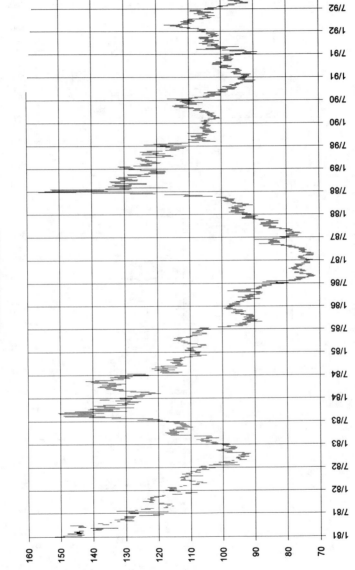

Meats Sub-Index

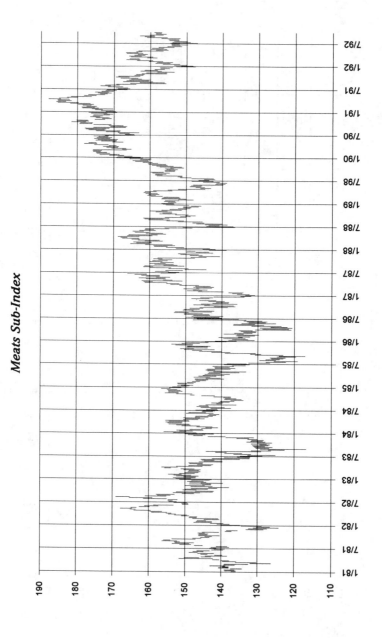

Metals Sub-Index

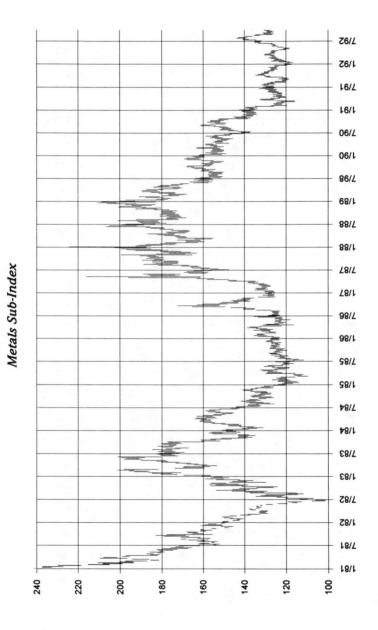

Food & Fiber Sub-Index

reflected in the WCI, to these other markets to determine where investors are placing their money.

Trading the WCI

Trading the Wasendorf Composite Index is simple in theory. First, we study the Composite Index to determine the overall trend. The trend is usually our friend and we want to trade in the same direction it is going. If the trend is up, we want to be long. If it is down, we want to be short.

Once we know the trend, we study the sub-indexes to learn which one or ones are most responsible for the direction of the trend. It is not uncommon for meats to be going south (down) and the grains north (up). The food/fiber index tends to be the most volatile of the sub-indexes and often leads the others from major lows and highs. It can start moving in a direction that the rest of the indexes will be headed a week or a month later. The reason is the markets that make up the food/fiber sub-index are thin, meaning low volume. When a market is thin, it only takes a little trading activity for it to make major price moves.

We have developed a set of simple ratios, which compare the individual indexes to the composite index. The sub-index value for each trading day is divided by the Composite Index's value for the same day (See Figure 5–3). If the ratio equals one, then the performance of the sub-index is the same or on par with the Composite Index. If it is less than one, the sub-index is below that of the WCI. If above one, the index is leading the Composite Index.

Another way of putting it is that the ratio tells us the strength of each index. This is of particular importance to us as we seek those markets that we want to trade. Once we know the trend and which group of commodities (meaning which sub-index) is most responsible for the trend, we look at the individual commodities within that sub-index to learn which commodities are making the strongest move.

Overbought versus Oversold Markets

Now we are approaching an area of critical importance to every trader. When is a bear market oversold, or a bull market overbought?

You want a trading system that gets you into a market early, allows you to profit from the trend, yet warns you when to take your profits and run. The Wasendorf System of Index Analysis is supposed to do this.

Figure 5–3
Ratio Chart of Grain Sub-Indexes to Composite Index

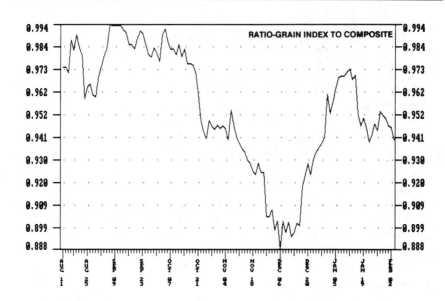

The price performance of each individual sub-index is compared to the Composite Index. This tells us which sub-index (or group of commodities) is leading and/or lagging compared to the entire Composite Index. By knowing this, we can easily spot the aggressive commodity(ies) in the entire group of 21. These are the ones that usually offer the most trading opportunity.

First, let's discuss the overall subject. It is nearly impossible to determine how far down a bear market will go down by how far it has already gone down. You can't always count on historical support to put the bottom in place, even if the price approaches zero. Once the commodity futures price of onions went below zero, lower than the price of the bags they were bagged in.

Now, we are not totally disregarding historical price information. Our indexes are built on it. Many traders follow the lows and highs, trading them as prices break trendlines. This action is responsible for the way falling or rising prices slow as major trendlines are penetrated. The point is simply that the terms "too low" or "too high" can't be used as a trading signal.

It was the subjectiveness of the terms "too low" or "too high" that prompted the development of a method to qualify the condition known as overbought or oversold. We observed that the nature of the markets is quite similar to the nature of the environment. Nature is not stagnant. You learn to understand it by reducing it to the averages of its extremes.

Take our concept of the weather as an example. Every night on the news, the temperature for any particular day is compared to the average temperature for that day and the historical highs/lows. This is one very important way of putting nature into a perspective you can deal with.

We put commodity markets into this perspective. Consider the idea of "normal." If you accept the premise of the balance of nature as an average of the extremes, then you can easily imagine "normal price" to be a narrow range, with prices through time quivering around that "normal" range.

Imagine a market beginning at a particular point. In Figure 5–4, we begin arbitrarily below a "normal price." At point "A" the price has approached the normal range and rebounded slightly. At "B" the price is within the normal range. At "C" a momentary quiver above the normal has occurred. "D," "E," and "F" are "A," "B," and "C" in reverse.

Although stylized, the pattern shown here is the nature of nearly all market price movement. You may see a resemblance of this pattern to the Elliott Wave Theory. Simplistically, the Elliott Wave is a study of prices quivering around normal. Incidentally, the range of normal does not need to be horizontal as illustrated. Normal can be trending higher or lower. The challenge now is to study the movement of price above and below normal in a statistical fashion. We wanted to create a method that was simple enough to calculate quickly while incorporating an adequate number of factors to be reliable.

A Moving Average Oscillator

Our final choice was to use moving average oscillators. If you calculate the value difference between two distinct moving averages (let's say, the price difference between a 20-day moving average of closing prices and a 10-day moving average), you'll discover that 10-day moving averages will be more sensitive to day-to-day movements while the 20-day moving average will be slower to respond. By studying the departure or the value difference between a longer and a shorter moving average, you'll discover how rapidly a price is moving away from normal and hopefully discover at what point the "rubber band" has stretched to its extreme.

Figure 5–4: Normal Price

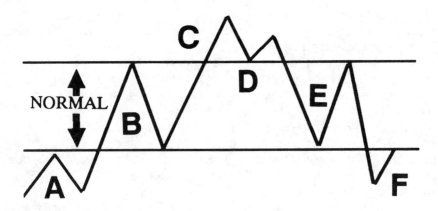

When thinking about the normal price of a commodity, you need to think in terms of ranges. Normal, for most commodities, is a moving target.

If you accept this argument thus far, then the final step is to determine the most appropriate moving averages to use. For our indexes, we chose a 10- to 20-day moving average oscillator for the short term and a 30- to 60-day moving average oscillator for the longer term.

Why These Oscillators?

The Short Term Internal Condition Indicator is an oscillator of monthly price action. There are approximately 20 trading days in a month. This indicator is designed to provide a view of the particular index, such as the Wasendorf Grain Index, on a relatively short term. It is useful as a confirmation of long term signals.

The Long Term Internal Condition Indicator provides a quarterly view of the market index, and is particularly useful because it shows how deeply the Market Index deviates from "normal."

The construction of these indicators may seem quite simple, nevertheless their accuracy has satisfied our needs over the years. Their usefulness, as a trading tool, also depends on following a set of rules and techniques.

The overbought/oversold indicators are designed to give you a view of the deviation from normal (See Figure 5–5). To better understand the application of rules regarding that deviation, it would be best to discuss the theories behind the rules.

Over time—be it 10 minutes or 10 years—the price of any commodity will vacillate on either side of "normal." The shorter the period being studied, the more likely the vacillation is meaningless "noise." On the other hand, studying a longer period of time provides more assurance that a true indication of a market's relative condition will be discovered.

The Ripples, Waves and Tide of the Market

Market "noises" were described by Charles Dow, as he constructed what is now the Dow Theory. Mr. Dow detailed three types of price action. For the purpose of this discussion, let's call them ripples, waves, and tides. Ripples of price action are the noise of the market and are, for the most part, insignificant to the overall trend. Intraday and day-to-day price action fall into this category. Dow considered these price actions to be untradeable because they were so short term.

"Waves" are the type of price action that reflect the market's reaction to mid-term phenomena, such as supply and demand changes, technical reactions, seasonal price patterns, and cycles. This price action is not only tradeable, it is often the only thing the average trader can trade in the futures market. They encompass a reasonably long time, usually greater than 30 days yet less than two years.

Market "tide" is the long term change in inflationary and economic factors. The "tide" of the market rises and falls in very broad sweeps—raising and lowering all the boats in the harbor. As the tide changes, nearly all markets change with it. Referring back to the Wasendorf Composite Index (Figure 5-2), you'll notice that from the second quarter of 1983 to 1987, the "tide" of the commodity markets was declining; and from the first quarter of 1987 to the middle of 1988, the market "tide" was rising. After that, it began another decline.

Figure 5–5: Overbought/Oversold Indicators

Short Term Internal Condition Indicator

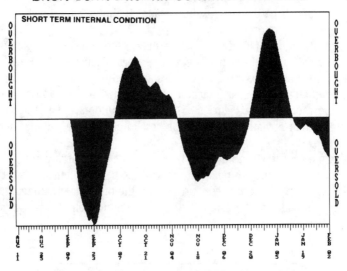

Long Term Internal Condition Indicator

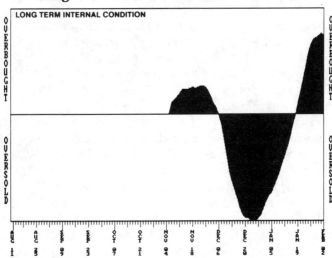

The Wasendorf Trading System uses long- and short-term momentum oscillators to anticipate price trend changes.

As we set our sights on the analysis of the futures markets, it is important to be aware of the "tide." But we are forced by market entry timing and money management considerations to trade the "waves."

The overbought and oversold internal condition indicators previously illustrated are designed to address market "waves." By segregating a short term wave from a long term wave, we can increase your ability to sell the crests and buy the troughs. From years of observing these oscillators, the following rules have evolved:

Rule Number One

The Long Term Internal Condition Indicator (LTICI) is the primary indicator. It tells us when a market has reached a low or high extreme when it turns from the oversold or overbought level, respectively. A turn is defined as a change in direction. If the trend of the indicator is toward the oversold, then a "hold short positions" signal is suggested. If this trend is stalled by the rounding of the pattern and then the values begin to become more positive, we have a buy signal.

Rule Number Two

The Short Term Internal Condition Indicator (STICI) is a fine-tuning instrument for the long term indicator. This is a lead/lag indicator. It will lead a sell or buy signal in the long term indicator, thus providing a warning of things to come. It may lag behind the long term indicator to provide confirmation of a signal. The short term indicator often makes several dips and rises while the long term indicator continues to trend. Therefore, it is critical to use the long-term indicator as the indicator of the overall trend.

Rule Number Three

The Long Term Internal Condition Indicator (LTICI) provides a buy or sell signal every time it turns, whether it has extended into the oversold or overbought area. This is true even though the indicator has rounded from the oversold and has not risen into the overbought. If it turns to trend into the oversold, this is a sell signal, and vice versa.

Rule Number Four

If the Long Term Internal Condition Indicator (LTICI) has turned, and the Short Term Internal Condition Indicator continues to move in the direction which was previously the direction of the Long Term Internal Condition Indicator, then the trader should wait until the short indicator turns before taking action. If the Long Term Internal Condition Indicator gives a buy signal, while the Short Term Internal Condition Indicator continues to move into the oversold territory, wait until the Short Term Condition Indicator turns before buying. These are examples of waiting for the short term indicator to confirm the long term indicator.

These rules provide signals for specific actions within the specific market group. The action prescribed is to buy the individual commodities of the market group if a buy signal is given (and/or to liquidate short positions). Of course, the reverse is true for sell signals.

The problem with the rules provided thus far is that the indication of a buy or sell signal provides no indication of the momentum of market movement. This is a traditional problem and is inherent to most technical systems and just about all fundamental systems. Furthermore, it is important to make a distinction between the momentum of price movement and the ultimate price objective.

The projection of price objectives is, in our opinion, a dangerous science. The danger is that seldom is a price objective met precisely. The expectation of a particular objective can cause the trader to overstay a position if the objective is not met, or to get out early if the objective is met and then exceeded. Simply stated: "You cannot tell how far down a price will go by how far it has already gone down, and vice versa."

In contrast to the projection of objectives, the forecast of market momentum can be a very useful tool. Momentum of a price movement refers to the speed of its rise or fall, and the inertia of its directional movement.

Certainly the speed at which a trade generates profits is a direct result of a market's momentum. More importantly, momentum is the most important factor for the long term trader. Strong momentum will hold a market in a long term trend. Weak momentum breeds consolidation—short term choppiness in the market that results in high commission expenses and numerous, usually individually small, market losses.

The anticipation of future momentum can be a valuable tool. If the momentum does not unfold as anticipated, then the likely outcome is market consolidation. If you have an effective tool to analyze the potential of momentum, then your extended profitability will more than finance your losses during the consolidation periods.

One way to view the potential for a market to gain momentum is to look at the extent of time a market is oversold or overbought. The longer a market is under or over "normal," the more tightly wound the main spring will become and the more likely the market will have a momentum movement in the opposite direction. The rule that relates to the anticipation of future momentum is:

Rule Number Five

If a market price movement causes the Long Term Internal Condition Indicator (LTICI) to make a double or triple dip into the oversold (or overbought) area without making a significant move into the overbought (oversold) area, then the likelihood increases for a momentum rally (or momentum decline).

Trade Selection Checklist

This discussion of the Wasendorf Trading System illustrates many of the characteristics that should be incorporated into the portion of your trading system used to select specific trades. Here's a checklist of those characteristics:

1. Choose an analysis procedure—or better yet, a series of analysis procedures—in which you have a high level of confidence.

2. Your analysis procedures should be qualitative and quantifiable. This means they must be specific in the sense they not only tell you to go long or short—but at what price or when.

3. Your procedures need to be able to withstand serious, historical testing. You must be able to go back into historical market data and run simulations. Your objective is to get an understanding of how your system performs in varying market situations, i.e., bull, bear, and sideways price movement. This can be done quite easily on today's personal computer systems. Actual results may not be the same as the hypothetical performance, though. The reason is simply that the pressure of trading (losing or making real money) modifies, for better or worse, our decision-making process.

4. Choose optimizable analysis procedures. This will help you avoid trading yesterday's factors in tomorrow's markets. Optimizing is a fine-tuning procedure. It does not mean abandoning your analysis principals. Opti-

mizing adjusts your analysis procedures based on a change in market conditions— such as a major change in market volatility—not a change in your trading system.

5. The analysis procedure should tell you when to get into a trade and when to get out. You'll want a procedure that can "admit when it is wrong," and tells you to take a small loss and try again.

Using the above checklist, our experience has indicated that computer-based systems fit the bill better than systems that are difficult to computerize. Computers take much of the opinion (or subjectivity) out of decision making and allow more accuracy in charting historical track records and hypothetical performances.

Don't forget the money management techniques we discussed earlier. You can't successfully trade if your system constantly drains your trading account of equity. Successful traders know they must survive the rough, choppy markets often encountered to be in a position to profit when the market smoothly trends up or down.

Surviving simply means preservation of your risk capital. You must be positioned financially and psychologically to withstand losing trades. You cut your losses quickly and let your winners run.

The trading system you select or develop should also have a definite procedure for protecting positions with stops or bail out points. It should have a mechanism for taking profits, and may have pyramiding procedures or position reducing principles included. The money management facet of the trading system should provide readouts of risk-to-reward ratios.

It is our opinion that money management is more critical than the analysis facet of the trading system. Even the best analysis procedure is seldom over 50 percent right. Good money management preserves your equity during the times that the analysis is wrong.

"Garbage In . . . Garbage Out!"

All trading systems demand information. You must feed them their daily ration of prices, open interest, volume, or whatever they use. It is critical that this information be accurate, timely, readily available and reasonably priced. If not, your system cannot function over the long term. The computer axiom "Garbage In-Garbage Out" applies to trading systems. If you don't input clean, accurate data, you can't expect reliable output.

A System Must Be a System!

The three components of a trading system described above must complement each other. They must work together to achieve a single goal. Your analysis, for example, cannot violate good money management principles. Also the data input must suit the analysis component. They must work like the Three Musketeers—"All for one and one for all!"

Worksheet 5

1. The three primary parts of a trading system are:

    A. _____

    B. _____

    C. _____

2. Which of these parts is the most critical?

    _____

3. Where does the Law of Probability come into play in futures trading?

    A. It's part of money management.

    B. It's part of diversifying your trading portfolio.

    C. It's not a part of either.

    D. It's part of both A and B.

4. A good futures trading system:

    A. Selects the right commodity to trade.

    B. Selects the right side (long or short) of the market to trade.

    C. Selects the right time to enter and exit the trade.

    D. Manages your equity.

    E. None of the above.

F. All of the above.

G. Only A, B, and C.

5. Explain the concept of market movement described as ripples, waves, and tides. Give examples and state what type of traders might trade each type of movement.

_____

_____

_____

_____

6. Discuss the importance of understanding the momentum of the markets you plan to trade.

_____

_____

_____

_____

7. What are the five universal characteristics of a trading system?

A. _____

B. _____

C. _____

D. _____

E. _____

8. Should you trade with "stops?" Why or why not?

_____

_____

_____

_____

9. True or False? The quality of the data you input into your trading system reflects in the output.

10. True or False? The most successful traders usually override the signals they get from their trading system.

Answers for Worksheet 5

1. The three primary parts of a trading system are:

   A. Researching and analyzing markets.

   B. Selecting specific trades including entry and exit points.

   C. Money management.

2. In our opinion, money management is the single most important facet of trading. If you can preserve your trading equity until you're in the right market on the right side at the right time, you'll be successful. Even the best analysis, results in losing trades 30 percent, 40 percent, and 50 percent of the time.

3. The answer is D. Use the Law of Probability to your advantage. Reduce your risks and increase your chances of catching a big winner by making as many and as diversified trades as practical.

4. The answer is F.

5. The concept of ripples, waves, and tides was popularized in the writings of Charles Dow and is the backbone of his theory regarding the price movement of the stock market. It applies equally well to the futures market.

   Ripples represent the very short term price changes—up and down trends that may only last a few minutes or hours. This is the province of the day trader and scalpers.

   Waves are what we think of as trends. They can be medium or even long term, lasting days, weeks, and even months. Most traders seek these price movements.

   Tides are the super-long term moves. They can last years and even decades. Because there is so much intermittent movement within tides, they are not tradeable.

6.   Momentum in trading is just as important as it is in business, school or sports. The market incorporates all the emotional energy of every person trading. It can be as fickle as the wind or as unrelenting as the ocean tide, and traders react to it just as dramatically.

You measure momentum various ways — volume, open interest, oscillators, RSI (relative strength index), etc. Like the trend, you do not want to be moving against the market momentum, unless you have a good reason. Otherwise, it will engulf your position(s).

7.   The five basic characteristics of the system you select to use to trade your futures account are:

A.   It must have your absolute confidence. Confidence gives you the perseverance needed to refine your system. A perfect trading system has never been developed—at least no one has shared it with the public. Therefore, systems require constant attention, if only to adjust to the dominant market patterns that are in flux.

B.   It must be specific. A system giving you vague signals is useless. You'll end up rationalizing your trading decisions and the results. You need to be able to clearly evaluate the results of the trading signals.

C.   It's just too risky, meaning expensive, to develop or purchase a system that hasn't been or can't be tested against historical data, although this is no guarantee that past performance will be an accurate indication of future results. Hypothetical results are often inaccurate and misleading. This is especially true when the pressure of losing real money enters the trading equation. On the other hand, if your system makes absolutely no use of historical data, we don't know how you will be able to have the amount of confidence needed to stick with it.

D.   It must be flexible and adjustable. The character of the market will change right before your eyes. A trend will start or stop. A market will begin moving sideways or sporadically up or down. A system that can't adjust must be abandoned.

E.   If your system doesn't cut your losses promptly, you won't survive long enough to learn whether it has any potential or not.

8.   We strongly recommend to our trading customers that they use protective stop loss orders. These are placed below long positions and above short positions. The reason is that there is no way of knowing if and/or when

markets will go against your positions. The hard part is often deciding exactly where the stop should be placed. It should be close enough to where the market is trading to provide protection, yet far enough away that the stop does not get taken out prematurely.

9. This is absolutely true. Never assume the data you retrieve from a service (CNN, Compuserve, Dow-Jones, etc.) or even from the paper (*Wall Street Journal, Investor's Daily,* etc.) is correct. Build in some type of data audit routine.

10. Most successful trades do not override their system, except under unusual circumstances. If you regularly second guess or disregard the signals you're getting, you don't have a system. Either you follow your trading system, or you find a new one.

6

Very Important Things You Should Know and Think About before Trading

---
Key Concepts

◆ Understanding the risk involved in commodity speculation.

◆ We have met the enemy and he is us!

◆ Completing account papers to open a commodity trading account requires serious thought.

This is a collect-all chapter covering some very important areas you need to be aware of BEFORE you start to trade futures.

First of all, commodity trading—including options on commodities or exchange-traded options—is a very speculative investment. Most traders lose. The

---

reason, in our opinion from being in the retail end of this business for over 20 years, is that most individuals are under-funded and/or under-disciplined.

As we mentioned earlier, when discussing survivability, even the best professional traders rarely have a trade success rate of over 60 percent. Most are happy if half their trades make money. Successful traders—the ones who are net winners—close losing trades promptly and let winning trades run as far as they can. Traders who lose characteristically hold losing positions too long, thus quickly diminishing their capital. Or, they only have enough equity to make a few trades. If one of these trades doesn't make enough money to pay for the losers, they are out of the market.

Therefore, to have a better than average chance to make money trading futures, you must be adequately financed. This means you have enough equity to diversify your portfolio, so you are in the *right* market, at the *right* time on the *right* side. Keep in mind that diversification can be a double-edged sword, especially if you don't understand the power of the leveraging created by futures contracts.

How Much Should You Leverage?

More importantly, how much is too much? Wasn't it Archimedes, the ancient Greek mathematician, who said that he could use leverage to move the world, if someone would show him where to stand? Since that time, circa 200 B.C., smart investors have done all kinds of interesting things using leverage. The commodity industry is a prime illustration of the art.

For example, a margin of $550.00 locks in 5,000 bushels of corn priced at $2.50 or so. That's a leverage ratio of 22:1. Or a $1,300.00 gold margin ties down $40,000.00 in this glittery metal—a 30:1 ratio.

But this isn't the only type of leveraging you need to be concerned with. We mention it because it helps provide a better overview of the entire leveraging picture. Another specific type of leveraging is the amount of leveraging you should do with the equity in your trading account. In other words, how many contracts, and of what size, should you acquire based on the size of your account?

For example, let's say you only have $10,000.00 in your trading account. How aggressive should you be? Our recommendation would be that you avoid leveraging it more than 15:1 and that new traders should stay closer to 10:1. This means that with the $10,000.00 trading equity, the value of the contracts you trade should not exceed $150,000.00 or $100,000.00 respectively. Here are a few examples:

$ Value of One Contract

Gold @$400.00/oz. × 100 oz. = $40,000.00

Silver @ $5.00/oz. × 5,000 oz. = $25,000.00

Corn @ $2.50/bu. × 5,000 bu. = $12,500.00

Soybeans @ $6.00/bu. × 5,000 bu. = $30,000.00

Oats @ $2.00/bu. × 5,000 bu. = $10,000.00

Live Hogs @ $0.50/lb. × 40,000 lb. = $20,000.00

Live Cattle @$0.70/lb × 40,000 lb. = $28,000.00

Crude Oil @ $20.00/bl. × 1,000 bl. =- $20,000.00

Sugar @ $0.10/lb × 112,000 lb. = $11,200.00

Cotton @ $0.60/lb. × 50,000 lb. = $30,000.00

Using the above numbers, it's easy to calculate the leverage ratio of a $10,000.00 account. With three gold contracts, it's 12:1; four silver 10:1; 12 corn 15:1; four soybean 12:1; 10 oats 10:1; 10 live hogs 15:1; five live cattle 14:1; five crude oil 10:1; 10 sugar 11:1; and four cotton 12:1. Keep in mind that the ratio constantly fluctuates as the price of the commodity increases or decreases. For example, if the price of soybeans increases to $8.00 per bushel, the ratio would change from 12:1 to 16:1.

When calculating the leverage factor of an account, new traders often use the margin required for a contract, rather than the total value of a contract. For example, let's say the margin for a COMEX gold contract is $2,000.00. If a trader used all the equity in the $10,000.00 account to buy (go long) five gold contracts with gold at $400.00 per ounce, the total value of the contract would be $200,000.00. This works out to a 20:1 leveraging factor, which is a little high and may be too risky.

With the above scenario, what happens if gold drops 2 percent in value, or $8.00? If you are long five contracts, the total value of the contracts declines from $200,000.00 to $196,000.00, but the equity drops 40 percent! The daily limit for gold is $25.00, or about three times the $8.00 loss discussed. Also, the trading range, and even the opening range, for gold can exceed 2 percent two or three times each year. A loss of 5 percent totally wipes out the $10,000.00 in equity, while a 5 percent increase doubles your equity.

For these reasons, we strongly recommend new traders pay close attention to the impact of leveraging. They should consider starting with at least $25,000.00 in equity—putting only half of that in the market at any one time. And, of that 50 percent, only risk 10 percent—better yet 5 percent—on any one contract.

This limits the commodities that can be traded and still gets some diversification. We recommend the mixture of grains, meats, metals, and food/fiber. You should follow two or three markets in each of these and trade only one or two in each complex. If there is $25,000.00 in the account and only half is committed to the market at any one time, that equals $12,500.00. If only 10 percent is invested in any one trade, the most margin to be used on any one contract is $1,250.00. At the present time, we don't want to exceed a 15:1 or 10:1 ratio between the total value of the account and total value of the contracts being traded. A portfolio might look like this based on the "$ Value of One Contract" table from the preceding page:

Commodity	Margin	$Value of Contract
2 Silver	$2,200	$50,000
5 Corn	$3,500	$62,500
2 Live Hogs	$2,000	$40,000
4 Sugar	$4,000	$44,800
	$11,700	$197,300

Here we are in four distinct market complexes. This gives us diversity, which in the futures market often equates to survivability and/or profitability. But, of course, you have no guarantee of either. The point is that you are spread out and have some reserve cash to cover margin calls if they should arise. The margin-to-dollar value of the portfolio is 16:1, a little on the high side for a novice investor. We might consider cutting back from four to two sugar contracts, for example. See Figure 6–1 for another example.

When you plan your portfolio, keep these ideas in mind. Your objective is to stay in the market, with as much protection as you can afford, until the markets run in your favor.

Figure 6–1: Sample Portfolio—$25,000 Equity

Tracking	Trading (# of Contracts)	Margin*	Contract Value
Grain			
Oats	1	$700*	$10,000
Corn	1	$700*	$12,500
Meats			
Live Hogs	1	$1,000	$20,000
Metals			
Copper	1	$1,000	$15,000
Gold	1	$1,300	$40,000
Food/Fiber			
Cotton	1	$2,000	$30,000
Sugar	1	$1,000	$11,200
		$7,700	$138,700

In this portfolio, there is $25,000 trading equity. Only half, or $12,500, is committed to the market at anytime. The ratio of the total value (based on "$ Value of Contract" table) of the contracts to the total equity in the account should be around 5:1 for new traders. It is 5.5:1 in this portfolio. And, the ratio of margin to total contract value is approximately 18:1.

*Margins constantly change. They are adjusted to reflect the volatility of the markets. Always check with your broker for current margins.

"Investor, Know Thyself"

One of the points the National Futures Association (NFA), the industry self-regulatory agency that oversees the conduct of commodity brokers, requires its members to stress when promoting commodity trading is that not every investor is suited for it. Trading requires a personality type that can withstand the risk, make fast decisions, and be very disciplined.

Are you suited to trading futures? One of the best ways to find out may be to read a book entitled *Your Inner Path to Investment Success: Insights into the Psychology of Investing* by Albert Mehrabian, Ph.D. (Probus Publishing Company, 1991).

The theme of Dr. Mehrabian's book is the matching of personality types of investors to various types of investments. It is not written primarily for commodity traders. It describes the psychology of all types of investors, from the most conservative to the most aggressive. Naturally, we slanted this summary of the book toward commodities, since that's what *this* book is about. You, and your non-trading associates, will find much more in it than the peripheral coverage you'll find here.

Dr. Mehrabian tells us there are two primary influences on our emotional response to the investments we choose. The first is internal, specifically our temperament or personality. The second is our "life circumstances."

We also have two choices to deal with—who we are and what we invest in. The first step is to get a fix on our emotional make up. Then, we can either match the type of person we are to the type of investment that best suits us, or we can understand the conflicts between the two and try to deal with them.

Dr. Mehrabian recommends matching personality to type of investment because the stress of failure—losing money!—evokes strong emotions in most of us, even the most analytical and rational. Once emotionalism seizes control, we can no longer consider ourselves investors. This loss of control can also occur because of the normal day-to-day course of business of certain investments. Contrast the machine gun tempo of commodity trading with the lackadaisical pace of a certificate of deposit in a federally insured institution.

Certain personality types can react just as illogically to a placid investment as a conservative investor reacts to a wildly unstable investment. The key is knowing your limits and working within them.

The book attacks this problem from two angles. The first thing it does is classify investments based on the level of uncertainty they possess. Commodity trading belongs on the high end because it is novel, complex, varied, changes rapidly, and makes many unexpected moves.

Then attention turns toward the investor. Temperaments are first divided into pleasant and unpleasant. The key is social expectations. The pleasant temperament has a positive outlook; the unpleasant type's expectations of social interchanges are negative. Most successful futures traders are found on the pleasant side of the spectrum.

The next classification is the arousable-unarousable temperaments. The arousable personality type, for example, is characterized as being emotional, volatile, energetic, expressive, and talkative. The unarousable is unemotional, stable, moderately energetic, and expressive. The unarousable can deal with high-uncertainty types of investments, like the commodity markets.

Dr. Mehrabian then describes the dominant-submissive temperament. As you'd expect, the dominant personality type appears strong, fearless, comfortable, relaxed, and does not hesitate to interrupt the speech of others. The submissive person comes off as weak, apprehensive, timid, uncomfortable and tense—shy would be a good description. Commodity traders tend to be dominant. They believe they have a certain level of control over their environment.

Once you have a firm understanding of these temperaments, Dr. Mehrabian mixes and matches them to create eight basic temperament types.

1. Exuberant = pleasant, arousable, dominant

2. Dependent = pleasant, arousable, submissive

3. Relaxed = pleasant, unarousable, dominant

4. Docile = pleasant, unarousable, submissive

5. Hostile = unpleasant, arousable, dominant

6. Anxious = unpleasant, arousable, submissive

7. Disdainful = unpleasant, unarousable, dominant

8. Bored = unpleasant, unarousable, submissive

From these classifications, most successful investors fall into the third group. They are optimistic, control their emotions, and believe they can be successful.

As we all know, people don't always fit neatly into categories. There's a big difference between the personality type that is extremely unpleasant or unarousable or submissive, and one that is a mild version of any of these.

Equally important is the impact of life's circumstances on our outlook, approach to investing, decision-making, and success. Life's circumstances are defined as all the changes and conditions associated with work, home life, or our extended family. For example, if tomorrow you win a $10,000,000.00 lottery, you would probably modify your approach to investing. Or, if you must deal—at home or at work—with a conflicting personality type day-in and day-out, you would probably have difficulty concentrating on your investing goals and strategies.

From what we've said so far about this book, we hope you've come to the conclusion that it can help you understand yourself, a relative, or an associate better. And, that this improved insight leads to greater success in the futures markets.

If you have any doubts whatsoever about whether you are psychologically suited for commodity trading, Dr. Mehrabian's book is must reading. The text is well written and easy-to-read.

Sign Away Your Rights . . .

Before being able to do any commodity trading, you must open an account with a brokerage firm. This requires filling out a set of account papers. We won't go over these in detail here, but we do want to alert you to some problem areas we found from years of dealing with individual traders.

The purpose of account papers is simple and direct—to let you know your rights and the risk you face. Since we already discussed risk, let's talk a little about the rights you assign to your brokerage firm, and the rules you must follow.

One of the most important rules is that you must maintain the correct amount of equity in your account at all times. This is called margin money.

There are two kinds of margins. The first is called the initial margin, the amount required when you first enter a position. The second is called maintenance margin. It is usually a little less, and is the amount you must maintain after a position has been opened. For example, let's say the initial margin for a given contract is $400.00. Once you are in the position, the maintenance margin may drop to $300.00. This means you must keep $300.00 in equity in your trading account for each contract you have acquired.

Now the equity in your trading account constantly changes and is calculated at the end of each trading day. This is called "mark to the market." For example, you have $1,000.00 in your account. You purchase one corn contract requiring $550.00 initial margin. You bought corn at $2.50 per bushel. This extends ($2.50 X 5,000 bushels) to $12,500.00.

If corn drops to $2.48 ($2.48 X 5,000 = $12,400.00), your account would be debited $100.00. Your equity is now $900.00. If the maintenance margin for corn is $500.00, the equity in your account could go down to that level before you would receive a "margin call." If corn continues to drop, you would eventually be on "margin call." For example:

Price	Contract	Loss	Equity
$2.50	$12,500	0	$1,000
$2.48	$12,400	$100	$ 900
$2.46	$12,300	$200	$ 800
$2.44	$12,200	$300	$ 700
$2.42	$12,100	$400	$ 600
$2.40	$12,000	$500	$ 500
$2.38	$11,900	$600	$ 400

As you can see from this table, once corn moves below $2.40, you start receiving margin calls. At $2.38 per bushel, you would get a $100.00 margin call. It is a "demand" for additional equity. Brokerage firms often require payment within a little over 24 hours, although some may extend this period depending on the size of the call and the past performance of the customer. The exchanges vigorously enforce margin calls to protect the integrity of the market.

The account papers you sign, when you open an account, give the brokerage firm the right to close your position(s) out if you don't make a margin call in the specified time. Then, even if your position returns to a profitable price level, you would still lose the amount of the margin call. For example, if you didn't respond to the $100.00 margin call when corn hit $2.38, your broker firm could offset your position and close your account. They would deduct the $100.00 from what was left in your account and send you the remainder. If corn jumped to $2.48—a limit up day—the next trading session, as you anticipated, you would still be out of the market.

Another aspect of margins you need to be aware of is that the exchanges reserve the right to change them without notice. They do this as a method of controlling trading activity. If trading becomes too wild, they can substantially increase the margin of a particular commodity or contract. This occurred in crude oil when Iraq invaded Kuwait in 1990, the Gulf War. The Chicago Board of Trade, for example, made 209 changes in margins in 1990 and 378 in 1989. Again, if you don't meet the new margin requirements, you'll be "taken out of the market" by your brokerage firm or its FCM. If you have T-bills on deposit, they have the right to "break" them to meet your margin, if necessary, as per the account papers you sign.

The margins are set each day by the margin sub-committees of the various exchanges. Each has its own particular system. You should check margins with your broker before initiating a new position.

Another area often causing problems for traders is their alternative for resolving problems that may occur with their broker or brokerage company. Included with account papers is a "Pre-Dispute Arbitration Agreement." First of all, it is an optional form. You do not have to sign it. If you do sign it, you agree to voluntarily submit your dispute regarding your futures trading account to an arbitration panel convened by the NFA. This could be a mixed panel, which means it could be composed of people within and outside the futures industry, at your request.

The benefit of signing this form is you can usually get a speedy resolution to your complaint without the cost of an attorney. The negative side is you may be waiving your right to sue in a court of law and you agree to be bound by the decision of the arbitration panel.

The NFA also provides a mediation service to help resolve disputes between its members (your broker) and customers. This is the first step and is not binding. You can call the NFA (1-800-621-3570) for an informational booklet.

If you have any questions, you should discuss them with an attorney who is well versed in security law. Also, keep in mind that the NFA is under the jurisdiction of the Commodity Futures Trading Commission (CFTC), which is a federal regulatory body similar to the Security and Exchange Commission (SEC). You can always petition them if you feel your arbitration has been unfair. Civil court litigation is always a possibility, but expensive legal fees usually accompany this option.

Our experience has been that if you have any problem with your broker, ask to speak with his supervisor. Most people in the futures industry work hard to keep customers pleased with their service. You will probably only have to turn to the more radical approaches as a last resort.

"Know Your Customer"

Federal regulations (CFTC) require futures brokers to "know their customers." The broker, along with his company and the firm that does the actual trading in the pits and holds the trading equity in escrow for the customer, have the joint responsibility of deciding if prospective customers are suited to the markets. To do this, they must gather certain information, the most important of which is financial data. The general rule of thumb is that a futures trader should be able to lose all of his investment without that loss affecting his/her style of living.

From a strictly business point of view, the futures commission merchant (FCM), the entity that holds your money and usually does the actual trading, wants to make sure you're good for your losses, if any should occur. With commodity futures, you are responsible for any loss you sustain, not just the amount of your investment. Conceivably, you could lose much more than the amount in your account. This can occur when a market limits up or down against your position(s). On limit days, little or no trading may take place as the market moves as far as it can, based on the exchange's rules. You may have a stop order placed to protect your downside risk, but the market price of the commodity you're trading can move right through your protective stop without any trading taking place. Until trading resumes, your position will not be offset and you will continue to lose money.

Now, if you do not or cannot meet your margin call, the FCM is responsible for putting up the money. They in turn look to the brokerage firm, usually designated as an introducing broker (IB). The IB usually looks to the individual broker (your broker) to make good on the debit. For all these reasons, everyone in the chain between you and the trading pits has a vested interest in your financial suitability.

What happens if you don't pay a debit? There is no single answer to that question. Much depends on the size of the deficit, the amount of trading you did, how much money there was made on your trading, the cost of recovery, and your ability to pay. Anything from a lawsuit to forgiveness could occur. It's no different than any other legal debt.

Some other important parts of the account papers you sign are:

◆ "Risk Disclosure Statement Acknowledgment." By signing this, you admit in writing that you understand all the risks involved in commodity trading.

◆ "Non-Cash Margin Disclosure Acknowledgment." Explains that you have been alerted to your rights regarding bankruptcy of the FCM.

◆ "Customer Agreement Acknowledgment." Here you state that you read and understood the customer agreement, which details all your responsibilities (like meeting margin calls) as a customer.

◆ "Permission to Cross" This makes you aware that your broker, some "associates" at his firm and at the FCM, may be on the opposite side of the market from you. They may be short a certain commodity futures contract when you are long. This shouldn't be a problem because there is always going to be someone on the other side of your trade. Commodity trading is a zero-based business. About the only time this can become a problem is when you ask your broker what his or her company's position is, and he is not truthful. If you lose money in this situation, you may have a complaint. But being wrong or giving you advice that loses money is not grounds for a complaint. We're dealing with the future and no one knows for sure what will happen.

◆ "Transfer of Funds." This gives the FCM permission to transfer funds from one of your accounts to another, if you have more than one, and if one is on margin call. This can occur, for example, when you have a securities and a commodity account at the same firm.

◆ "Options Risk Disclosure Statement." When you sign this, you acknowledge that you understand the risk involved in options trading.

These aren't all the forms, and not all of these are required by each FCM. For example, if you are a hedger, opening a corporate account, trading foreign markets, or giving trading discretion in your account to a third party, you'll be asked to sign even more forms and/or releases.

Keep in mind the following when you read—and before you sign—these forms. First, they detail the maximum risk you will encounter. Secondly, they were written to satisfy CFTC regulations. And, last of all, they were prepared to protect the FCM and the brokerage firm, as much as they protect you. After a careful reading, you should have no doubt about where you stand.

Worksheet 6

1. True or False? Most traders lose money trading futures and options on futures.

2. True or False? You can make a profit in the futures market if half or more of your trades lose money.

3. Explain how leveraging can help commodity traders make exceptional returns on the money they invest, and how this same factor adds to the risk or speculative nature of commodity trading.

4. What are the major categories of physical commodities?

   A. _____

   B. _____

C. _____

D. _____

E. _____

5. You diversify your risk capital investment in futures because

    A. It's a good money management technique.

    B. It provides the opportunity to survive and prosper.

    C. It's a good approach if you're not sure which market to trade.

    D. It's a guarantee of success in the futures market.

6. True or False? Every investor is suited to trade the commodity markets.

7. Is your personality or temperament suited to trading futures? Explain.

_____

_____

8. True or False? Margin money is a down payment of a futures contract.

9. True or False? A margin call is a simple request for more trading equity. It does not have to be honored.

10. True or False? The futures industry has several good methods to resolve customer complaints.

11. True or False? Having a protective stop loss order behind your commodity position assures that you can get out of your position if the market moves against it.

12. True or False? The only reason for the account papers is to make you aware of your rights and the risks you will face trading futures or options on futures.

Answers to Worksheet 6

1. This is correct. There is an interesting book on the subject entitled *The Commodity Futures Game: Who Wins? Who Loses? Why?* by Richard J. Teweles, Charles V. Harlow, and Herbert L. Stone. Chapter 13 reviews the best known studies that have been done on this subject.

2. The answer is true. Your objective, as a speculator, is not to have best won and lost record. It is to become a big net winner. You should care less whether half or more of your trades lose. What you must concentrate on is sound money and portfolio management so you are in the right market on the right side at the right time. Let your winners run, cut losses promptly.

3. Leveraging enhances return on investment because you are controlling a large amount of a commodity with a small amount of money. For example, the initial margin for a 5,000 ounce silver contract may be $1,100.00. The value of the contract, when silver is at $6.00 per ounce, is $30,000.00 or a leveraging factor of over 27:1. Silver only has to increase $0.22 or about 4 percent to double your money on one long silver contract.

   The opposite, or risk, side of this equation is equally impressive. A 4 percent decline in price would equal a 100 percent loss of the margin money.

4. The major categories of physical commodities are:

   A. Grains

   B. Meats

   C. Metals

   D. Energies

   E. Food/Fiber

   Grains and meats are sometimes combined in "agricultural" commodities. Petroleum contracts, crude oil, gasoline, heating oil, are sometimes grouped with the metals or extractables (commodities that can be extracted out of the ground). The food group, of the food/fiber category, may be broken off and called the "softs" or the "breakfast" (coffee, cocoa, sugar) commodities.

5. The answer is A and B. You diversify your risk capital investment in commodities because there is no way of absolutely knowing when or where the next major move will occur. Diversification additionally enhances your chances of survival.

6. False. Commodity trading is a highly speculative investment, not suited for every investor.

7. You'll have to answer this one for yourself. We include it in this worksheet because it is so important a consideration.

8. False. Margin money is a good faith deposit, not a down payment.

9. False. A margin call is a demand that additional equity be added to your account. If you ignore it, your position and account may be closed. You would still be legally responsible for any unpaid balance in your account after your account is liquidated.

10. True. This is one of the advantages of investing in government regulated investments.

11. False. A protective stop is a good precaution, but should never be considered a guarantee that you will be filled (offset) at your stop price. The market could make a limit move through your stop. If a market is locked in limit moves, no trading takes place.

12. False. Warning you of the risks you face as a commodity trader is a very important function of account papers. But you must keep in mind that they also protect your broker, his company and the firm clearing the trades. Therefore, understand them from this point of view as well.

7

Computerized Trading

Key Concepts

◆ Understanding the value and limitations of computer-assisted commodity trading.

◆ Basic types of trading software programs.

◆ Using the "ideal system" for software selection.

◆ Description of some useful programs.

Now, we'd like to provide you with some insights into the state of the art regarding the use of computers by the individual trader. Computers have found a permanent role in futures trading because they can increase your feeling of control, and reduce anxiety. We recommend them because they can do a lot of the menial number crunching and research for you—freeing time up for money/management and studying the market. But we are getting ahead of ourselves. Let's start at the beginning.

Why Consider Computerization?

People have been successfully trading using pencil and paper since the Chicago Board of Trade began in 1848. In the late 1950s, electronic calculators were added. It wasn't until the late 1970s that individuals started using computers.

Does Everyone Need One Now?

Of course, the answer is no. For example, individual traders, who are fundamentalists, would find it very difficult to build an econometric model, particularly on a personal computer (PC). The size and complexity of these models require mainframe computers and enormous amounts of expensive data—all out of reach of most individuals. Fundamentalists could use their PCs to access fundamental world news and weather information. Or they might create spreadsheets or specialized programs to help them track the supply-demand equation, or a single aspect of the fundamental situations. The computer, in this case, would only be another aspect of data input, rather than the heart of this trading approach.

The technicians are more inclined to build their systems around computer software, but again, it is not a necessity. Traders who use a simple system, like tracking concurrent moving averages or point-and-figure charts, can easily update several markets daily on paper. Those who analyze chart formations can update their charts daily and do their analysis without the need for computers.

Nonetheless, two critical movements, one independent of the other, were underway in the 70s. The first was the development of the personal computer's speed, memory capacity, graphics, and user friendliness, to a point where a large number of traders could afford them and, more importantly, operate them. Concurrently, the popularity of commodity trading was growing dramatically.

These two trends encourage the development of software for PCs. This gave individual traders more confidence in their ability to analyze the markets, making them competitive with floor traders and other professionals. To accommodate this increase in interests, new contracts and retail firms evolved.

These trends also strongly influenced the institutional side of the market. Actually, this side of the business led the retail. Institutional traders had access to one or more PCs or work stations, often linked to mainframes. They hired programmers to develop proprietary programs for their corporations.

The individual traders had champions as well. One of the earliest and best known was Tim Slater, who founded the now famous Technical Analysis Group (TAG) in 1978. It is probably safe to say Tim has done more than just about anyone else to promote technical analysis on PCs.

TAG developed a program, or more correctly, gathered a series of technical analysis programs, that eventually became CompuTrac. In the beginning, it appeared to be a bit piecemeal. One study was added to the system at a time. Whenever you received a mailing from them, something more had been added. Back then most of the work was being done on Apple computers. It was just about the only option at that time widely available to individuals. Eventually, the system migrated to the IBM-DOS platform.

What Is the Motivation for a Commodity Trader to Purchase and Use a Personal Computer?

1. **Discipline.** A good computerized trading system can help you tame your impulses. Successful traders, in our experience, rely on their system and follow its rules. They are controlled and systematic, not wild and unrestrained. Software is no substitute for a stable personality, but at times it can slow down someone who is overly emotional.

2. **Education.** Many of the software packages available do an excellent job of teaching traders how the market reacted to past events, providing insight into what to expect in the future.

3. **System Testing.** If you have an idea how you'd like to trade a market, you can simulate past markets and evaluate or fine-tune your approach.

4. **Saving Time.** Properly managed and structured, a computerized system can reduce, for example, the time it takes to update 40 markets each day from hours to minutes. Another good example is the calculation and recalculation of complex equations, like the one for the RSI (relative strength index).

5. **Historical Perspective.** With a few key strokes on many systems, you can view a long-term or short-term chart of a specific market. This can often be done simultaneously with multiple windows on a single screen.

6. **Ease of Analysis.** Sometimes it is just easier to do certain types of analysis on computer. Examples would be drawing Gann lines and

squares, or calling up the meaning of all the individual Japanese candle-sticks and the multiple formations.

7. **Second Guessing.** Some traders review various computerized studies to make sure they aren't missing an important signal.

8. **Paranoia.** Technical analysis can be a self-fulfilling prophecy. A quick review of various technical studies gives you an insight into what others in the market are likely to do.

This is not a complete list of the advantages. But we do hope it gives you an idea of the edge computerized technical analysis can provide.

Which Software/Hardware Is Right for You?

Before you can select the hardware (CPU, modem, CRT, memory, printer, mouse, etc.), you must know what software you will be using. For example, if you choose a trading system that runs on IBM-DOS operating systems, you may not be able to run the program on a UNIX or Macintosh operating platform. Equally important are the attributes—such as speed, memory size, and screen quality—of the system you select. Many of the complex trading programs are memory hogs. They demand a lot of random access memory (RAM) and read only memory (ROM). Or, a high resolution color monitor might be a requirement to distinguish between the many lines, such as Gann squares or angles, used in the analysis process.

Before you purchase any software, you must decide how you are going to make your trading decisions. How does computerization fit into your trading system? Does it drive your trading, or will you use some software as an auxiliary tool? To aid you in this process, we'll now discuss what we consider the major classes of software for the futures trader.

Black versus White Box

The first way we classify trading software is whether it is black or white box. Black box programs are not fully disclosed. They perform a specific function(s), but that's all you know. Additionally, you cannot make any adjustments. You acquire these programs to satisfy a specific need or answer specific questions; you can make few or no changes.

It's common for this type of program to be trendy. They get "hot," work for a while, then fade into obscurity. We think the reason is that they handle one type of market, such as a trending one. Once that changes, the program no longer works. It cannot adjust or be adjusted by the user.

Another problem we have with these black box specials is that it is very difficult for someone to design a program for someone else. Therefore, many people buy them, only to find them unusable for their system or trading tactics. Also, certain trading approaches work for one market, but not for all markets. Which markets are the right ones for a particular software package?

From time to time, we have found a use for certain of these programs. You might want to find one that complements your basic trading system. It could provide you with confirmation of what your system tells you. Let's say your system alerts you to a buying opportunity in soybeans. You also have a program that analyzes Japanese candlesticks. It has been reliable, from your research, in the bean market. You double check it to see if the current candlestick formation is bullish. That's one way to use these black box programs.

Or you may have a program that predicts seasonal patterns. You double check it to make sure you are not bucking a seasonal trend before you place a trade.

White box programs, on the other hand, provide in-depth explanations of the analysis, how it works, often including formulas, and instructions on adjusting or modifying the output. They are flexible, allowing you to adjust to changing markets and your trading style. You drive the software, rather than the software driving you.

Naturally, there is much middle ground, the "gray" programs. These permit minor changes and adjustments. One of the ways to distinguish between black and white is the amount of instruction you get from the program and documentation. The more you learn, the whiter is the box. If you get nothing from the program but an answer, it's a black box for sure.

Neither is necessarily right or wrong. It's your needs that count. In some cases, all we want is a reliable answer. In other cases, we want to learn all there is to know about an analytical technique, then be able to customize it for our own use.

Single versus Multiple Programs

Computer programs can do a single function, or they can take the tool box approach by providing many technical studies. This applies to either black or white box type applications.

A typical black tool box program might, for example, provide price charts. On these charts, you could overlay moving averages, relative strength indexes, Gann lines, etc., by pushing a few keys. You would have a very limited ability to make any modifications to what is available. Some of these services can be very extensive in the studies they provide. They are like supermarkets where you pick and choose whatever you need depending on the situation. This is the type of information that is often available from services that provide live (actual time) quotes.

The quintessential white tool box program, in our opinion, is CompuTrac. It includes over 65 programs ranging from relatively simple open interest studies to very complex ones, like Williams %R or his "Ultimate" Oscillator (Reference Figure 7–1). The documentation alone could be considered a definitive study on technical analysis.

Our last classification includes programs designed to assist you in developing your own trading system. They fall into two basic types. The first is what is known as an expert system, which attempts to mimic a master. You feed your trading rules and experience into the system. It then takes the data and does the analysis. You constantly fine tune the operation and it even "learns" on its own by combining the rules or lessons of the expert. These are very sophisticated programs.

A variation of this approach is the neutral network. These programs manipulate data with the knowledge of the desired output in hopes of finding the rules or patterns. They require much patience, time, and experience.

Which approach suits your needs? Only you can answer that one.

Selecting Trading Software

So far we discussed why you should consider computerizing your trading, and the general classes of software available. Now we'll explore a method of selecting the software that suits your needs.

The Ideal System

There is an approach to problem solving that also works well for selecting software. It's called the "Ideal System." What you do is let your imagination run wild. You ask yourself: How could I ideally solve this problem? If I had no financial, internal political, or personal restraints, what would I do? You then write down the ideal solution to your problem.

Figure 7-1: Computrac's Programs

Advance-Decline	Normalization
Alpha-Beta Trend Channel	Norton High/Low Indicator
Andrews Pitchfork	Notis %V
Arms Ease of Movement	Oil Crack Spread
Average True Range	Open Interest
Black-Scholes Option Analysis Module	Oscillator
Bollinger Bands	Parabolic (SAR)
Bolton-Tremblay	Percent Retracement
Commodity Channel Index	Planets Module
Commodity Selection Index	Point and Figure
Compression of Data	Quadrant Level Lines
Crocker Charts	Rate of Change
Cutler RSI	Ratio
Cycle Finder	Relative Strength Index (RSI)
Demand Aggregate	Schultz A/T
Demand Index	Shift
Detrend	Soybean Crush Margin
Directional Movement	Spread
Envelopes	Standard Deviation
Fibonacci Fanlines, Arcs & Time Zones	Stochastic (%K, %D)
Fourier Analysis	Stoller STARC Bands
Gann Lines	Swing Index
Gann Square of Nine	Tirone Level Lines
HAL Momentum	TRIX
Haurlan Index	Trading Index
Herrick Payoff Index	Trend Lines
Linear Regrssion	Volatility
Moving Average Convergence/	Volume
Divergence (MACD)	Volume Accumulator
McClellan Oscillator	Wave
Median Price	Weighted Close
Momentum	Williams %R
Moving Average	Williams "Ultimate" Oscillator

Once you have brainstormed the situation and outlined the best of all possible approaches, you begin to compromise with reality. What can you afford to do? What can you live without? What do you have time to do? What restraints are real and which are imaginary? How can you circumvent some of the limitations? What's left?

The rationale for this approach is that this exercise often opens new avenues of thought. You find unique and valuable approaches you may have previously overlooked. It's not uncommon that some of these new insights will substantially improve the solution you eventually reach.

To apply the Ideal System concept to the selection of software, you prepare a list of all the features you ideally would like to have as part of the software you want. This becomes your checklist as you evaluate potential packages. To keep you in touch with reality, you can mark those that you feel are absolute necessities. Here's an example:

Software Features Absolutely Necessary [X]
   Live Price Quotations [ ]

Chart Formations
   (Trendlines, Channels, etc.) [ ]

Basic Studies
   (RSI, Moving Averages, etc.) [ ]

Advanced Studies
   (Gann Lines, Williams %R, etc.) [ ]

Unlimited Studies
   (100+ basic & advanced) [ ]

Artificial Intelligence
   (Expert System) [ ]

Neutral Network [ ]

Historical Testing Capability & Data [ ]

Portfolio Analysis [ ]

Risk-Reward Ratio Calculator [ ]

Spread Sheet [ ]

News [ ]

Weather [ ]

Fact Database [ ]

Order Placement [ ]

There isn't room here, but you could make a shopping list of the hundred-plus individual studies, programs, functions, and accessories currently available. Then check the ones you feel fit into your trading system or style of trading.

Your objective is to clarify your thinking. How are you going to select trades? Entry, exit points? What tools do you absolutely need to make these decisions? How much information do you need? How automated are you going to be? Will you input price quotations live? Daily? Manually? Are you a day or a position trader? Are you going to look to your system for money management assistance, as well as trading? Will you maintain your trading diary on computer as well? Can you communicate your orders to your broker electronically?

Once you ascertain what you want or need, reality sets in as you price out your selections. A quote system providing on-line price ticks with a decent variety of studies runs $300.00 to $500.00 per month. Additionally, you may have to add something to cover the transmission of the signal (cable, satellite dish, dedicated telephone line, FM antenna), depending on where you are geographically located. A white tool box type of program, like CompuTrac 3.21, costs between $695.00 and $1,895.00, depending on which modules you acquire. A single study program, like "Candlestick ForeCaster," goes for $249.00.

If you would like to have price quotes but can live with a 10 or 15 minute delay, there are reasonably priced (under $50.00 per month) alternatives. DTN and Farm Dayta are examples. The delay allows you to get the quotations without having to pay each exchange a fee, varying from $30.00 to $50.00 per month. Four futures exchanges could cost you $150.00 to $200.00 in exchange fees alone.

Research Your Choice

Let's say you narrow the field to a half dozen programs that meet your needs. What do you do next?

The first thing we recommend is to visit, if possible, someone who is using the system in a way similar to how you plan to use it. Does it really work the way the promoters claim? Can it provide the information you vitally need to trade successfully?

Next, find out if the software has been battle tested. Who has traded commodities using the software? Make sure you distinguish between real time action, as opposed to simulated or hypothetical trading. For a variety of reasons, most importantly our human emotional responses to pressure, it is not uncommon for historical simulation to look great, while live action falls flat. Some trading approaches appear to be automatic, but in real life trading requires a flow of decisions.

Get a tight fix on two critical inputs—your time and money. Many programs require daily highs, lows, opens, and closes. Some may additionally ask for volume and open interest. How is this data to be inputted? If the answer is electronically, what computer format does the program support? If you have an on-line quote system, will the software accept the data directly, or is conversion necessary? If so, is it expensive or even available? The last thing you need is a program you can't update easily and inexpensively.

Always research the user friendliness of the program and customer support supplied by the vendor. The easiest-to-use programs today provide pull down menus and support a mouse. Also, check the hours customer support is available compared to when you will normally be using the program.

We always like to have an insight into how many times the program has had major upgrades. This is usually a whole number change in the version, version 1.0 is superceded by version 2.0. Minor changes often are recorded by a decimal change, version 3.5 is replaced by version 3.6. Beware of version 1.0, it may still have some bugs to be found and corrected. Check to see if you get free upgrades when the software is improved.

Always try to get a demonstration diskette, preferably one that runs the program on some limited basis, as opposed to a one that creates a computerized slide show. The actual running demos provide a much better insight into what the program does, and how it feels to you.

Caveat Emptor

"Let the buyer beware!" If it sounds too good to be true, it probably is. Therefore, don't order anything that doesn't have a good guarantee. Also, use your credit card, so if you don't like what you get, you can send it back and refuse to pay the charge.

There really are some excellent, well-written programs available. It just takes time and research to find them.

Worksheet 7

1. List five reasons individual commodity traders might want to consider using personal computers as part of their trading system.

    A. _____

    B. _____

    C. _____

    D. _____

    E. _____

2. True or False? White box software is better than black.

3. True or False? You get more for your money with multiple purpose software programs than those that provide only a single technical program.

4. True or False? PCs lend themselves to fundamental analysis.

5. What are the key areas to consider when selecting commodity trading software?

    _____

    _____

    _____

Answers to Worksheet 7

1. Here are some reasons to consider using a PC (personal computer):

    A. May provide discipline.

    B. Can help you learn how to trade.

    C. Allows you to test trading systems, approaches, strategies.

    D. Saves time, particularly in performing tedious calculations.

    E. Provides historical perspective.

    F. Makes some types of analysis simpler.

2.   False. It doesn't matter if software is white or black box. What matters is whether it satisfies the need you have.

3.   False. Single purpose software is often more expensive on a per technical study approach. But the key to value is buying only what you need. Often with multiple study software, you buy some technical analysis programs that you do not need or want.

4.   Personal computers do not lend themselves to fundamental analysis. The serious econometric models are too large for these machines. They can be very helpful in creating supply-demand balance sheets or accessing weather and other news services that impact fundamental analysis.

5.   The key areas to consider in the selection of software to assist you in trading commodities are:

   A.   Your needs. What do you need from a software program? Review the check list created using the Ideal Approach. Does the software fit your trading system?

   B.   How, and at what cost, will the program need to be updated based on daily trading activity of the markets to be tracked?

   C.   Once you get a fix on the program(s) that appear to meet your needs, what are the hardware requirements?

   D.   Does the program(s) suit your personality? Are you comfortable with it? Do you understand it? Will you be able to easily use and keep it current?

8

Twenty-One Golden Rules to Profit By

Key Concepts

◆ How the rules impact your trading—whether you follow them or not.

◆ Successful trading demands discipline.

◆ Twenty-one rules to help create discipline.

Now let's switch direction for a while. In our opinion, rules inspire discipline—the single most important characteristic any trader can possess. If you don't have a written set of trading rules for yourself, you should prepare one.

Why Learn the Rules?

Like any profession, a body of rules has evolved over the years for commodity traders. You need to learn the rules for two reasons. First, they give you a good

---

insight into what other traders can be expected to do when faced with traditional circumstances. Commodity futures trading, by its very nature, deals with the unknown. Since no one really knows what will happen next, many tend to stick with the rules and move with the crowd. If you can sense the direction of the herd and move with it or ahead of it, you can make a good living as a commodity trader. This is how a trend following system works. The only caveat is that the market must be trending, which is not always the case.

The second reason to learn the rules is to know when to break them. This is the essence of contrarian trading. These traders zig when everyone else is zagging. They look to short bull rallies to going south when everyone else is headed north. Contrarians often do well in choppy, trendless markets. Plus, if they are right, they can catch trends just as they begin and exit before they reverse.

Trend followers, on the other hand, often miss or lose a portion of each move. For example, let's say they are long one of the metals—silver. It has been trending slowly higher for the last six weeks, moving from $5.00 an ounce to $5.25. That's a gain of $1,250.00 (5,000/oz. × $0.25) per contract. When the move stalls, trend followers must wait to see if the trend is actually changed, or if silver is going to go higher after some sideways movement. If the trend has changed, it may drop a nickel or so before the trend change is confirmed. In other words, they give up $250.00 (5,000/oz. × $0.05) waiting for confirmation. They probably lost approximately the same amount at the beginning of this move, as they waited for confirmation that the move had begun.

The life of contrarians isn't any easier. They often catch moves early, but in the process often get whipsawed. That's when they trade a false start or move. The market moves in their direction temporarily, only to move violently against their position. In other words, they are prey for false moves. They may also get out of moves too soon, if they misread or get a false signal.

There is no simple, surefire route to trading success. Knowing and understanding the following rules—even if you choose to ignore one or more of them from time to time—can help. At least you'll have an idea of what the professional traders are considering as they face the same situation.

We'd like to begin with some very general—almost philosophical—principles. Then we'll get more specific.

1. Rule Number One contradicts all the ones that follow—**Be a Doubting Thomas!**

    First off, don't believe anything you hear about trading. Use all you learn as a guide, and find out what works for you as an individual trader. This frame of mind spills over into what your broker and fellow traders tell you is going to happen in a particular market, or their advice in general. We have seen a lot of people make a lot of money in the commodity markets, but we've only seen few, if any, who made money consistently by listening to someone else. The basic rules, combined with your education, experience, and understanding of your markets, blend into a unique approach. This is your trading system, which includes money management and psychological restraints, as well as your trade entry and exit decisions.

2. **Be totally open.** Open to new ideas, new strategies, new markets, new information, new forms of trading and communicating. Never forget you're attempting to predict what will occur at some point in the future. Most traders assume price patterns repeat, but exactly when and how closely the patterns mirror past ones is unknown. Look for the old, but trade the new.

Your approach to the markets should include the flexibility to change your mind. Or to trade the short side of a market as well as the long. To make adjustments in your money management or trading system. To consider markets you haven't previously traded. A successful trader is often the one aware of the most options or alternative paths. They have the flexibility of a master chess player to adjust to the unexpected.

3. **Be well aware of who you are.** Trading commodities is 90 percent mental and the other half is knowledge and experience, to paraphrase a famous baseball saying. Know your level of risk tolerance; you won't make sound decisions when you're way over your head financially. Nor when you're too tired or ill or not prepared to trade. Don't be afraid of missing an opportunity by taking a day off. Believe it or not, there are always great new trades in the offing. Learn to be patient; pick and choose your trades carefully.

Match your personality and temperament to your trading system. If you're not a detailed person, use a system that doesn't require any. If you're very excitable, avoid day trading. Consider being a position trader and, once you put a position on, let it alone until you're ready to offset it.

4. **Diversify, young man, diversify!** Think about diversification on many levels. To begin with, commodity trading should represent a small portion of your entire net worth. Allocate 10 percent to 20 percent of what you consider risk capital. This is money, that if you were to lose all of it, would not affect your lifestyle.

Next, you need enough trading equity to give yourself a better than average opportunity of being in the right market on the right side at the right time. Having the resources to trade only one market at a time limits your odds substantially. Additionally, you need enough reserves to withstand setbacks and losses. Some very serious investors even like to further diversify by diversifying into some type of professionally managed commodity trading program besides the account they personally trade.

There is also the concept of negative correlation to consider. This is the backbone of Modern Portfolio Theory. Negative correlation occurs when one market or investment class (stock, commodities, real estate, etc.) moves up compared to another that is moving down. For example, there is a negative correlation between the stock market and the commodity markets. Negative correlation, properly used, is desirable because it smoothes out the performance of an investment portfolio.

5. **Place your markets in their historical perspectives.** Even if you don't use them as signals or indicators, you should know the historical highs and lows of the markets you trade. Additionally, you must have a good understanding of the seasonal patterns and major cycles. Why? Simply because a large number of technical traders will trade based on these patterns. You must take their anticipated reaction into account as part of your overall trading analysis. If, for example, you go long corn into what are the normal seasonal lows (at harvest), you better have good reasons or deep pockets.

6. **The same reasoning, expostulated in Number Five, applies to developing a sound knowledge of technical analysis.** It is often called a "self-fulfilling prophecy" because so many traders see the same technical signal and react in unison. For example, an uptrend line is broken alerting technical traders that the current uptrend is now a downtrend. Just like a herd of longhorns heading for water, they stampede to the short side of the market.

7. **Don't spit into the wind, trust a junkyard dog, or trade contrary to the trend.** There are good psychological reasons trends are created and maintained. For instance, would you pay more for something you intended to resell if you didn't think it was going to increase in value? Of course not. You go long a market because you believe you'll be able to

sell the commodity for more in the future. The same is true of a down trending market. You sell because you think you'll be able to buy or offset your positions at a lower price.

The amazing thing is that this is nothing but human nature. We all feel this way. Just about all traders trade this way, causing markets to trend.

Therefore, you need to know the trend of the market you are about to enter before you open a position. You can either go with or against the trend. If you go against the trend, you need a good reason—such as that it is about to enter an area of resistance you feel it cannot penetrate, or you become aware of some fundamental information that is not yet in the market, but has the potential of turning it around. Either way, you want to know what the herd is thinking, what the trend is.

8. **Develop a definite plan or strategy for entering and exiting trades.** For example, you might enter a market with limit orders and exit by continually moving your trailing stops closer to the trading range until they are hit. The danger you want to avoid is not carefully planning entry and exit points. All too often, traders get in markets too late and exit too early. Or novice traders get filled "unexpectedly" and have no idea what to do next, nor any strategy planned to exit the trade.

9. **Part of your trading plan should include a risk array analysis.** This makes you aware of the down side risk you are facing. The first part of this array is locating areas of support for long positions and resistance for short positions. Next, you need to evaluate how strong or dependable these support or resistance points are. For example, let's say you are planning to take a long position in the silver market at $6.00. Your analysis leads you to believe silver will move to the $6.50 area, a gain of $2,500.00 per contract before transaction costs, over the next three to four weeks. But what if you're wrong? What if it moves lower?

By studying the long, mid and/or daily price charts (or using some other type of analysis), you pinpoint areas of support at $5.95, $5.86 and $5.84. This simply means that past downward movements in this market slowed, stalled, or stopped at these prices. Therefore, you assume they may again. This analysis highlights $5.86 as the most reliable of the support areas. Therefore, you calculate your downside risk at $0.14, or $700.00.

Your expectations (or best estimates) are $2,500.00 gain versus $700.00 loss, or an over 3:1 reward to risk ratio. This is an acceptable range.

One last consideration you need to be aware of is daily trading limits. For silver, it is $0.50. This means silver can move against your position $0.50, or $2,500.00 without trading in a single day. And, a commodity futures contract can make limit moves for more than one day in a row. Limit days occur when there is a lot of volatility in a market, caused by uncertainty, fast breaking news (rumors)—the unexpected! To complete your risk array analysis, you must factor in the possibility of limit moves for or against your positions. Calculating this unknown is a value judgment you make from experience and all the information available.

10. **Guard against over-trading.** There are two situations where traders are particularly vulnerable—right after they have just made a big gain or lost. If they have just pocketed a major gain, they feel omnipotent. They are invulnerable. They can't make a mistake. They believe every trade they pick will be a winner. On the other hand following a substantial loss, some traders become desperate to earn back their loss. Their trading becomes wild, erratic. It's called the "double or nothing" syndrome.

In either case, the trader has lost the discipline needed to rationally trade. The best thing to do is take a "trading holiday." In other words, just stop trading for a day or two (or longer if necessary) until the warm glow of success or the pain of failure passes. Then, go back to the markets as if the event never occurred.

11. **Don't let profits become losses.** This may sound obvious, but it is a common problem for many traders. Variations of this axiom are never hold positions too long and avoid the temptation to pick tops or bottoms. What often happens is traders become greedy, once their positions become profitable. Instead of taking profits when available, they cling to trades. Eventually, as all markets do, trends change direction. Since bear moves tend to be faster than bull moves, prices often plunge. Before traders with profitable long positions realize it, the profits disappear and the positions are losers. The same can happen to traders holding out to close long positions at the top or shorts at the bottom.

If you wait too long to take profits, you'll often regret it—not to mention what this strategy does to your nervous system. An approach mentioned earlier, of following profitable positions with protective trailing stops, can help resolve this character flow. Remember—"Bears win and bulls win, but hogs get slaughtered!"

12. **A corollary to the previous rule is avoid closing positions prematurely.** We've seen experienced traders very orderly open a position and precisely close it when their price objective was hit. We tell our customers: "You can't tell how far a market is going up (or down) by how far it has gone already." The only true way of knowing is when it changes direction and is no longer going up or down. Following positions with protective stops also corrects this problem.

13. **Learn the art of placing protective stops.** It is easy to tell you to place stops, but it is not as easy to tell you how or where. It requires much experience with the specific markets you trade and a good feel for the current and expected volatility. You need to place your stops close enough to where your position is trading to protect yourself from losing what you've gained so far, yet not so close that you get prematurely stopped out. In other words, if the commodity you are trading has had a day range over the past few weeks of $0.04, you would place your stop at least outside of this range (above for short positions and below for long). Additionally, you'll need to know where the support and resistance levels are, and if there were any technical signals that could influence other traders.

    For example, if your market has been trending upward along a 45-degree angle for the past three weeks, many traders will be following it. If this trend line is broken, these traders will probably react to it by going short, driving the market down further. Therefore, your stop should be closely following this trendline. If you get stopped out and are still bullish, look for a point to reenter. Where would this be? It can often be found at the next support or resistance level.

    Your objective in placing stops is to protect yourself if your analysis is wrong and/or to avoid giving any profit back to the market once it is earned. At the same time, you want to avoid being whipsawed.

14. **Try not to overtax your resources, particularly time.** Carefully evaluate how much of a commitment in time, money, and mental resources you can make. Most part-time traders should avoid day trading because

they can't sit in front of a quote screen during trading hours. Also, day trading takes a lot out of one emotionally; there's nothing left some days for your regular job.

Part-timers should limit themselves to tracking three to five markets and trading only two to three. The markets should be ones that you have some prior experience with, a special interest in, or are knowledgeable of through your profession or life experience. For example, traders with farm backgrounds often have a good feel for the agricultural markets. Trading markets you're fond of makes the research easier.

15. **Plan and develop rules for taking profits.** For example, don't exit a market just because you've become bored with a trade. On the other hand, if a market moves dramatically in your direction and you have no idea why, take your windfall profit or at least put a tight stop behind the position. Part-timers should never buy or sell to get scalping profits (these are small, short term profits). The reason is that it takes too much time to follow the markets close enough to be successful on a regular basis. Scalping is the province of floor traders, who pay very low commission rates because they are members of the exchanges. Part-timers should be position traders, holding trades for several days, weeks, or months.

16. **Learn to short the market.** The majority of new and part-time traders go long. Most of us are just more comfortable buying a commodity at a given price and selling it for a profit at a higher price. We seem to find it foreign to our thought process to sell something we don't have and later buy it. Commodity trading is a zero-based business, which means for every gain there is a loss. The short side of the markets can be just as rewarding as the long. Keep in mind that bear moves last about half as long as bull moves and that the use of stops is just as important.

17. **Never hedge "trade" or try to spread out of losses.** True hedging occurs when you are on both sides of a market. The correct way to do this is to be on one side of a cash market and on the other side in commodity futures. For example, a farmer has 5,000 bushels of soybeans in a storage bin or growing in his fields. In other words, he is long 5,000 bushels. To hedge, he sells 5,000 bushels on the Chicago Board of Trade. He is now neutral pricewise. When the commodity contract is about to expire, he can deliver the beans or offset his position. The rationale for hedging is to pass the risk of ownership to a speculator and lock in an acceptable profit.

Some commodity traders, when faced with a losing long position, sell a short on another exchange. They call it hedging, but it isn't. It's more like an intermarket spread. This is bad trading. When faced with a losing position, offset it and take your loss. If you wish to trade spreads, do so. Look for spread opportunities when the relationship between two related contracts is, by your analysis, misaligned. If you decide to reverse your position, do it. But do it as a completely new trade.

18. **Never go long just because a commodity's price is low, or short because a price seems high.** Traders often get trapped by the logic that, if a commodity is below the cost of production, it must go higher. This may be true in the long run, but it sure isn't in the short to medium term. Remember the old onion contract that went below the cost of the bags in which the onions were packaged. Silver is often a by-product of lead and other base metal mining. Its production can continue after its price drops below production costs. Even the cattlemen continue to produce livestock when in the red. For example, it takes two and a half years from the time a cow is bred until a steak is produced from its offspring. This process can't be turned on and off at will.

Consequently, if you shorted the silver market in early 1980 because it was "too high" at $30.00 an ounce, you would have regretted it as this commodity shot up over $10.00 more an ounce.

19. **Never leg out of a spread, unless this was your original strategy.** Legging out of a spread means selling off one side and continuing to hold the other. For example, let's say you notice the gold-to-silver ratio is over 90:1. It takes 90 ounces of silver to buy one ounce of gold. You think this is high and should return to a level of 60:1 or 70:1. Therefore, you decide to enter a spread. Your analysis indicates silver should gain on gold, reducing the spread. Therefore you go long silver and short gold. To get a better balance dollarwise between the two commodities, you decide to go long two silver contracts and short one gold per spread.

You are in a legitimate spread for legitimate reasons. Therefore, when you close out this position, you should offset both legs. Sometimes inexperienced traders see both gold and silver increasing in value. They adjust by offsetting the short gold and holding the long silver contracts, or even reversing the short gold to a long gold. The purpose of a spread is to profit from the changing relationship between the two commodities. In this case, the trader expects silver to move farther and faster than gold, while being protected from adverse bearish moves in metals by being short gold. It is generally considered a more conservative play than holding net long positions in both commodities.

There is nothing wrong with being net long or net short. It is just a completely different trade than the spread and should be entered that way. You can get yourself in trouble by making changes and adjustments midstream. Most times, you are better off backing out of any trades that are not working, taking your losses, and beginning new trades fresh.

20. **Learn the risks and rewards of pyramiding.** This is the use of unrealized profits on current commodity positions as margin for more positions, unusually in successively smaller increments. For example, let's say you are long 10 crude oil positions. The price goes up $2.00 per barrel. You think it is going even higher. You add five new positions with your paper profits. Your analysis is correct and you add two more positions with additional new profits. It still moves higher, so you add one more. You build a pyramid with a base of 10 contracts, then five, two, one. Thus the name.

The risk is, of course, giving into greed and holding the positions too long. You're buying new positions with unrealized (paper) profits. If the market turns against you, you now have 18 contracts, not the initial 10. The last eight were purchased at prices substantially higher than the initial 10. These are more vulnerable to negative price activity.

The reward is that you are increasing your leverage. The initial margin money required to purchase 10 contracts now controls 18. If you exit with a profit on all contracts, your reward-to-equity ratio will be spectacular. On the other hand, if the crude oil market goes against your pyramid, it could be devastating.

21. **Self-discipline—the ultimate key to successful futures trading.** If you learn nothing else from this material, this is the most important single aspect. Here are a few tips:

◆ Create a comprehensive trading strategy. This includes money management as well as a trading system. Put it in writing.

◆ Money management is the more important of the two.

◆ Never trade when you are sick—physically or psychologically.

◆ Follow your own trading system. Avoid the advice of others. If you want someone else to make your trading decisions, give them the discretion (limited power of attorney) to do it.

◆ Set break periods. For example, if you have three or five losses in a row, it's time to back off for a while.

◆ Keep a journal explaining why you entered each trade, why you exited, the results and a critique of your performance. Compare what you actually do to your initial money management and trading strategy.

◆ Try not to procrastinate. If you select a trade, do it. If you're hesitant, don't.

Give serious consideration to these Golden Rules. Commodity traders are working for themselves. Trading is a business at best, an investment at the least. It requires the same attention and devotion your employer expects from you on the job.

Worksheet 8

1. Of the 21 rules listed, which five appear to be most useful?

   A. _____

   B. _____

   C. _____

   D. _____

   E. _____

2. True or False? A written set of trading rules is only for novices.

3. True or False? The most experienced traders offset one side of a spread at a time.

4. Define the term "trailing stops." How are they used?

   _____

   _____

Answers to Worksheet 8

1. All are important. You must study them and select those that are most meaningful to you intellectually and psychologically.

2. False. Writing clarifies thought and nothing needs clarification more than your trading rules. Every investor should take the time to write out his/her rules.

3. False. This is called legging out of a spread and can be very dangerous, unless this was the original strategy. Normally, you offset both legs at the same time.

4. Trailing stops are market orders used to offset current positions. They are placed below long positions or above short positions. The purpose is to protect the position, if the market moves against it or to close out profitable positions automatically when the market trend changes.

9

Preparing for the National Commodity Futures Examination

Key Concepts

◆ What is the NCFE?

◆ Who should take this exam?

◆ How to pass the NCFE.

◆ A sample test helps prepare traders for the markets.

The National Commodity Futures Examination (NCFE) is just one of a series of exams individuals can take to become qualified to satisfy the registration requirements of various states, federal, or industry regulatory agencies. For example, to

---

become registered to sell real estate, one must pass a state test and register with that state. The same is true for lawyers and doctors.

To become a commodity broker, you must pass NCFE and register with the National Futures Association. As the name of the test and association imply, registration is on a national basis, as opposed to statewide.

The NFA is an industry self-regulatory organization (SRO). It receives its authority from the Commodity Futures Trading Commission (CFTC) and is supported by commodity traders. An NFA fee is assessed against every trade executed on any of the commodity exchanges. When you trade, you'll see this charge on your statements.

Traders new to the commodity markets often ask whether they should take this test. Its purpose is to determine if a commodity broker candidate has a basic understanding of the markets and the regulations governing the industry.

For several years, we were directly involved in conducting Commodity Education Institute's week long schools, which prepare brokers to take the NCFE. Most of the participants were people who planned to become brokers. At each class, there were always a few individuals who attended with the purpose of obtaining industry background before trading.

The NCFE is divided into two major sections. The first covers market knowledge and trading; the second tests familiarity with the rules and regulations governing the industry.

Some of the subjects covered in the first part are:

◆ *General Theory.* Development of futures market, cash market versus futures market, cause and effect of price volatility, elements in cost of storing commodities.

◆ *Hedging Theory.* Risk, effects of hedging on working capital, income, purchasing costs, and profits.

◆ *Speculative Theory.* Speculative trading's effect on market liquidity and price volatility, leveraging.

◆ *General Contract Functions.* Transfer of ownership, forward contracts versus futures contracts, delivery premiums, and discounts.

◆ *Options' Terminology.* For example, in the money, at the money, out of the money, delta, puts, calls.

◆ *General Futures Terminology.* For example, basis, bucketing, churning, cost of carry, open interest.

◆ *Margin Requirements.* Initial and maintenance margin for hedging, speculating, and spread transactions. Who has authority to establish minimum margin requirements? What does margin represent? How are margins determined?

◆ *Option Premiums.* Intrinsic value, time value. Effect on components of premium as expiration date approaches.

◆ *Price Limits.* What happens when a futures market trades up to the daily maximum? How does this affect margin?

◆ *Offsetting Contracts.* Procedures for settlements and deliveries.

◆ *Options Exercise, Assignment, Settlement, Process of Assignment, Exercising/Offsetting Puts and Calls.* How are gains and losses calculated?

◆ *Types of Orders.* When they are used, restrictions on use of certain types.

◆ *Price Analysis (Fundamental and Technical).* How different aspects of the economy effect futures prices, supply and demand, yield curves, charting.

◆ *Basic Hedging.* Buying hedge, selling hedge, bona fide hedging, calculating basis.

◆ *Hedging Commodities.* Grains, livestock, food/fiber, metals, energy, lumber, financial markets.

◆ *Spread Trading, Applications.* Common types of spreads, risk associated with them.

◆ *Profit/Loss Calculations.* For speculative trades, including spread trades, and trading applications for all the major commodity and futures contracts.

◆ *Option theories.* Strategies and techniques.

The second part of the exam tests regulatory compliance issues:

◆ *Regulations.* Registration, opening a customer account, risk disclosure statement, customer funds, position reporting requirements, speculative trading limits, confirmation of option/futures transactions, customer complaints, disciplinary proceedings.

◆ *CPO/CTA General.* Registration, customer monies, fees, and commissions, account statements.

◆ *CPO/CTA Disclosure Documents.* Performance table, trading history, business background, rules for filing.

◆ *Disclosure Requirements.* CPOs and CTAs are required to notify customers of "up front" fees and organizational and offering expenses, while FCMs (futures commission merchants) and IBs (introducing brokers) must disclose all costs associated with futures transactions.

◆ *Know Your Customer Rule (NFA Rule 2-30).* Risk disclosure statements or documents required by rule, information required to be obtained from customers.

◆ *IB General.* Rules for accepting customer funds, capital requirements, time-stamping, risk disclosure acknowledgments.

◆ *General Account Handling and Exchange Regulations.* Commodity Customer Agreement form, registered representative's ("RCR") employment with more than one firm, collection of margins by RCR, customer disputes.

◆ *Discretionary Account Regulation.* Requirements for an AP to handle discretionary accounts, forms required for discretionary accounts.

To pass, broker candidates must obtain a score of 70 percent or more on each part. If a failing grade is made on either section, the entire test must be retaken. Candidates are allowed two and one-half hours to answer the 120 questions.

The exam costs $75.00 each time it is taken and is administered by the National Security Dealers Association (NASD). The majority of people take the test on a computerized system available in most parts of the country, but special arrangements can be made for a written exam.

It has always been our feeling that attending a school and taking the actual exam was overkill for someone who only plans to trade commodities, as opposed to brokering them. But studying a broker manual or home study guide isn't a bad idea. These provide excellent overviews of the industry, market knowledge, and regulations. If you would like to get a feel for your chances of passing the NCFE, try the sample one in Worksheet 9.

How Should a New Trader Get Started?

First thing to do is take a cold shower. Don't do anything in a hurry and don't let any broker convince you that you need to act fast. The greatest thing about commodity trading, in our opinion, is there is always a good opportunity coming down the pike. If you miss today's "incredible trade," be patient—there'll be another one tomorrow.

Once you have yourself under control, honestly answer the following questions:

1. Am I emotionally stable enough to trade commodities? ( )Yes ( )No

   This is a critical question. If you are very excitable or can't control your greed, you'll regret trading commodities. The market or a broker will be able to manipulate your feelings. This leads to poor decision making.

2. Am I intellectually prepared? ( )Yes ( )No

   Do you know enough to trade? About the specific markets you wish to trade? About the mechanics of buying and selling commodities? About how to get the information (news, price quotations, etc.) you need for your trade selection? About your broker and his/her firm? About how the industry is regulated?

   If not, what can you do about it? You've made a good start with the purchase of this book. And, there are many others you may want to read. Also consider trading schools and seminars. Your broker should be a good source, as well. All the exchanges have customer educational programs; contact their public relations or public information departments. Then there are hundreds of newsletters and just as many software programs, many of which simulate trading. There are even a few industry magazines. We additionally recommend you begin a paper trading program. Learn for yourself if you have a nose for picking winners.

3. Am I financially suited? ( )Yes ( )No

   As discussed earlier, commodity trading is a highly speculative investment. Only risk capital should be used. A minimum amount is, in our opinion, at least $5,000.00, but we prefer $25,000.00. You need to be able to survive some drawdown in equity to be in the right market, on the right side, at the right time.

4. Am I prepared to do the hard work required to be a successful trader? ( )Yes ( )No

   Trading profits are generated over the long term from a combination of research, money management, rational decision making, and perseverance. You don't just stumble into an unbelievably profitable trade the first time you trade. You must develop a trading system, nurture it, feed it data, fine-tune it. At the same time, you balance your equity to use it in the most efficient way. Add to this the emotional roller coaster as you move from profits to losses to profits to losses—with each incline and drop getting steeper.

The research alone exhausts some traders. There are reports to read and analyze, charts to update, journals to be kept. Most successful traders have a flair for details. They can recite when the last highs or lows were of the contracts they trade; which formations are reliable. They know where to get the confirming data needed.

We're not trying to discourage you. Our point is simple, that futures trading is a serious business. If it were easy, everyone would be doing it. There just can't be an investment where someone can double, triple, or quadruple their money in a matter of days or weeks without a few catches.

Therefore, be prepared to use your gray matter. Think defensively. Move cautiously. Finally, we wish you the best of luck.

Worksheet 9 (Sample NCFE)

1. The effect of speculation is to:

   A. Increase price fluctuations

   B. Alter supply to demand forces

   C. Reduce farmer risk in growing his crop

   D. Reduce the range of cash price fluctuations

2. The major distinction between cash and futures contracts are:

   A. Offset procedure

   B. To-arrive positions

   C. Inspection procedures

   D. Commodity grade

3. The concept of futures trading was used in Europe long before U.S. markets were developed.

A. True

B. False

4. A cash forward sale is essentially the same as a futures contract with the major difference being the ability to offset in futures.

A. True

B. False

5. Cash forward and futures contracts differ in that:

A. The latter are traded on organized exchanges, while the former are not

B. Futures contracts are standardized and cash forward contracts are frequently negotiated

C. Futures can be more easily offset

D. All of the above

6. The motive of the speculator is profit.

A. True

B. False

7. The efficiency of a market is most influenced by:

A. The number of traders

B. The weather

C. The availability of cash supplies

D. The amount of margin requirements

8. On the purchase or sale of a futures contract, transfer of ownership is not accomplished unless:

A. 50 percent of the cash value of the contract has been deposited.

B. The commodity position is offset.

C. The commodity is actually delivered.

D. It is done via a regulated commodity exchange.

9. The cash market and the nearest futures contract tend to converge:

A. At the country elevator

B. At the end of the month

C. At terminal markets

D. During the delivery month

10. If a futures contract is offset, delivery is required immediately.

A. True

B. False

11. If a farmer wants to hedge his crop, he would buy futures.

A. True

B. False

12. The most important function of a futures market is:

A. Forward pricing

B. Attracting speculators

C. Assembling, standardizing, and grading

D. Eliminating all risk

13. About 98 percent of all futures contracts are satisfied by offset and not delivery.

A. True

B. False

14. The owner of an option on a futures contract must:

A. Offset his/her position

B. Exercise his/her position

C. Take delivery on the expiration date

D. None of the above

15. Without a futures market in which to hedge, the price of a loaf of bread probably would be:

A. Higher

B. Lower

C. Makes no difference

D. Always stabilized

16. In selling futures against a growing crop, one is said to be assuming the role of a:

A. Speculator

B. Hedger

C. Spreader

D. Gambler

17. Anybody who is engages in a business that is subject to price fluctuation is a:

A. Hedger

B. Scalper

C. Processor

D. Speculator

18. A hedge position:

A. Eliminates chance of profit

B. Increases need for working capital

C. Shifts risk to another

D. All of the above

19. To hedge against a forward cash sale you would:

A. Sell futures

B. Make a substitute sale

C. Buy futures

D. Arbitrage

20. An individual who does not own or have access to storage facilities should not trade in futures.

A. True

B. False

21. A short hedge protects against:

    A. Rising prices

    B. Falling prices

    C. Both technically

    D. None of the above

22. When buying or selling a futures contract, one is contingently liable for:

    A. Original margin

    B. 70 percent of total contract value

    C. Total contract value

    D. None of the above

23. A cash forward contract differs from a futures contract primarily in that:

    A. A cash forward contract is usually more personal.

    B. A futures contract can be more easily offset.

    C. The cash contract is the result of arbitration.

    D. A futures contract is almost always the result of open outcry.

24. The function of the speculator is to provide liquidity.

    A. True

    B. False

25. A commodity futures short sale may be made:

    A. By anyone at anytime

    B. Uptick

    C. No tick

    D. Downtick

26. A cash sale can involve a forward contract.

    A. True

B. False

27. Which of the following is not considered a part of carrying charges?

    A. Storage costs

    B. Interest

    C. Transportation

    D. Insurance

28. Hedging may be defined as "the marketing strategy of offsetting the risk of price fluctuation inherent in any cash market position by taking an actual, but opposite, position in the futures markets."

    A. True

    B. False

29. When a futures contract is offset, delivery is made immediately.

    A. True

    B. False

30. When a futures price is more than the cash price, the market is called:

    A. Inverted

    B. Reverse

    C. Discount

    D. Premium

31. A person who holds an inventory would hedge by:

    A. Making a substitute purchase

    B. Making a cash forward purchase

    C. Entering into a "to-arrive" contract

    D. Selling futures

32. A put option is considered "out-of-the-money" when:

    A. The broker executes the option

    B. The customer offsets the option

C. The strike price is below the current market price of the underlying futures contract

D. The strike price is above the current market price of the underlying futures contract

33. The term "ex-pit" is essentially the same as "against actuals" (AA) and "exchange for physicals" (EFP).

   A. True

   B. False

34. Hedgers will usually pay a smaller margin than speculative longs and shorts.

   A. True

   B. False

35. A selling hedge at a full carrying charge premium is almost always worthwhile because:

   A. It gives price protection regardless of whether prices subsequently rise or fall

   B. When prices are rising, the value of spot usually rises more than futures

   C. When prices are falling, the value of spot usually declines less than futures

   D. An adverse basis change is unimportant

36. Cash and futures prices will tend to converge during the delivery month.

   A. True

   B. False

37. Trade margins are usually lower than those for speculative customers because:

   A. They are subject to smaller price fluctuations

   B. They are financially more stable

   C. There is less risk in their position

   D. The statement is not true

38. A "put option" gives the owner the right:

A. To a profit in the futures market

B. But not the obligation to a short futures position at a pre-specified price

C. But not the obligation to a long futures position at a pre-specified price

D. Pick the strike price desired

39. Cash transactions always involve forward contracts.

    A. True

    B. False

40. A grain elevator operator who hedges generally intends to deliver against a futures contract he sells.

    A. True

    B. False

41. A hedger who is long a contract of December wheat has in effect made a(n):

    A. Substitute sale

    B. Inverted hedge

    C. Substitute purchase

    D. Speculation

42. A futures hedge involves having a short futures position when one owns the cash commodity and a long futures position when the cash commodity is needed.

    A. True

    B. False

43. With a buying hedge in futures:

    A. Interest costs on money used to finance inventory tend to be greater

    B. Working capital needs are smaller

    C. The hedger usually will accept delivery of the commodities tendered so as to minimize his costs

    D. Basis changes are not important

44. A buy hedge would be used by:

A. A farmer to protect his crop

B. A grain elevator operator to protect his inventory

C. An exporter to protect his sales

D. None of the above

45. Hedging techniques only work effectively for the short term.

A. True

B. False

46. A hedge position may not give full protection against adverse price movements because:

A. During the time the hedge is operative the basis may change

B. Cash prices and futures prices usually move in unison

C. The various futures months do not usually sell at the same price

D. Transportation costs vary from one area to the next

47. Options on futures and commodity contracts cannot be traded together.

A. True

B. False

48. If a seller delivers against his short future position with better than contract grade, the buyer may be required to pay a designated premium for it.

A. True

B. False

49. Unless offset, a contract calls for delivery of a specific quantity and grade(s) of a commodity.

A. True

B. False

50. A delivery notice issued by a short constitutes a change in ownership of the cash commodity.

A. True

B. False

51. The buyer has the right to demand delivery at any time during the delivery period.

    A. True

    B. False

52. An order to buy five May wheat on the Chicago Board of Trade placed with one broker and a simultaneous order to sell five May wheat on the Chicago Board of Trade placed with another broker is:

    A. An intramarket spread

    B. An intermarket spread

    C. An intercommodity spread

    D. A wash sale

53. A grain elevator operator receives delivery of three million bushels of wheat on May 1, for which he pays $4.00 a bushel. At the same time, he enters into a commitment to buy an additional 1,000,000 bushels for delivery on June 1 at $4.10 a bushel. The elevator operator would most likely:

    A. Hedge 3,000,000 bushels on May 1 and 1,000,000 bushels on June 1 by buying futures

    B. Hedge 3,000,000 bushels on May 1 and 1,000,000 bushels on June 1 by selling futures

    C. Hedge 4,000,000 bushels on May 1 by buying futures

    D. Hedge 4,000,000 bushels on May 1 by selling futures

54.
Date	Cash	Futures Price (July)	Basis
10/3	126½	145¾	−19¼
1/3	131½	145¾	−14¼

    What is the net basis gain for a sell hedger using the period October 3 and January 3?

    A. −5

    B. Nothing

    C. +3/4

D. +5

Use the following information to answer Questions 55 and 56:

The price of cash on August 1 is $2.20.

The price of September futures is $2.30.

The price of December futures is $2.40.

55. If a hedger who is long on the basis were to sell September futures, his basis would be:

A. $0.10 over

B. $0.10 under

C. $0.20 over

D. $0.20 under

56. If a hedger who is short on the basis were to buy December futures, his basis would be:

A. $0.10 over

B. $0.10 under

C. $0.20 over

D. $0.20 under

Use the following table for questions 57, 58, and 59.

Date	Cash	Futures	Basis
Oct 1	149½	159½	−10
Nov 3	149¼	162½	−13¼
Dec 1	151	160	−9
Dec 24	160	184	−24

57. If someone who needed a cash commodity bought futures as a hedge on December 1 and liquidated the hedge on December 24, the hedge would have contributed how much profit to his operation:

A. +15

B. +24

C. +9

D. No profit; in fact, a loss

58. If the sell hedge was established on November 3 and liquidated on December 1, the results would have been:

A. +2 1/2

B. +4 1/4

C. +1 3/4

D. +3 1/4

59. If the cash commodity was owned and if futures were sold as a hedge on October 1 and liquidated on November 3, how much would the hedge have contributed or cost with relation to his carrying charges:

A. −3 1/4

B. +3 1/4

C. −13 1/4

D. −3

Use the following information to answer questions 60, 61, and 62.

Date	Cash Oats	Jan Oat Futures	Basis
July	1.35	1.50	−15
Sept	1.40	1.40	0
Dec	1.42	1.47	−5
Jan	1.43	1.40	+3

60. For an oat elevator operator, how much would a hedge placed in July and lifted in September contribute towards carrying charges?

A. −$0.05

B. −$0.15

C. $0.05

D. $0.15

61. How much if placed in September and lifted in December?

    A. −5 cents

    B. −15 cents

    C. +5 cents

    D. +15 cents

62. How much if placed in September and kept to expiration?

    A. −$0.05

    B. 0

    C. $0.03

    D. $0.13

63. A lumber dealer enters an order with a mill to purchase lumber for delivery in three months, with the price of the lumber to be based on the price on the day of delivery. The lumber dealer hedges by buying futures. The price of futures is $204.00 and the price of cash is $210.00. On the day the cash lumber is delivered, the price of the cash lumber is $214.00 and the price of the futures is $220.00. The hedge resulted in a:

    A. $6.00 profit

    B. $6.00 loss

    C. $10.00 profit

    D. $10.00 loss

64. A spreader who is bullish on a commodity would consider:

    A. Selling the near and buying a deferred month

    B. Buying the near and selling a deferred month

    C. Cannot calculate his spread risk

    D. None of the above

65. Spot, cash, physicals, and actuals all refer to essentially the same thing.

    A. True

    B. False

66. In a normal market where the difference between more distant and near futures contracts in the same commodity, for example July corn vs. December corn, is expected to narrow a spreader would:

   A. Buy near future, sell distant future

   B. Avoid trading futures under these circumstances

   C. Take no action

   D. Sell short

67. A spreader who has purchased December wheat and sold March wheat on the same exchange has established:

   A. An intermarket spread

   B. An intercommodity spread

   C. An interdelivery spread

   D. A commodity product

68. The interdelivery (or intramarket) spread is the most popular spread.

   A. True

   B. False

69. If the near month is at a premium over the far month and you expect the spread tomorrow, you would as a spreader:

   A. Buy the near and sell the far

   B. Enter into a limited risk spread

   C. Sell the near and buy the far

   D. Sell the far and buy the near

70. In a spread position:

   A. There is always a predictable risk

   B. There is only a limited profit opportunity

   C. There is no limit to the risk involved when you sell a near and buy a far month

   D. Carrying charges always prevail between a near month and a far month

71. Speculators normally avoid a thin market.

    A. True

    B. False

72. An intramarket spread requires there be no more than one market.

    A. True

    B. False

73. Exchange traded options are priced:

    A. By the exchanges on which they trade

    B. By open outcry in trading pits, just like futures

    C. Between the owner and the seller

    D. By dealers and brokers

74. A spreader who sold March corn and bought May corn when futures were inverted, would have:

    A. Unlimited profit potential

    B. Unlimited risk

    C. No profit potential

    D. No risk

75. Spread positions usually require less margin because:

    A. Price changes between futures months are less than flat price risks

    B. The two months involved always move up and down together

    C. There is virtually no risk

    D. All except A

76. Pyramiding is the practice of using accrued paper profits as margin for additional trading positions.

    A. True

    B. False

77. The purchase of May wheat in Chicago and sale of May wheat in Kansas City is an:

    A. Intermarket spread

    B. Interdelivery spread

    C. Intramarket spread

    D. None of the above

78. An individual who simultaneously buys soybeans and sells oil and meal has effected a reverse crush spread.

    A. True

    B. False

79. Exchange traded options are risk-free investments.

    A. True

    B. False

80. A call option is said to be "in the money" when:

    A. The broker gets paid his commission

    B. When there is high demand for it

    C. When the underlying futures contract is trading above the strike price

    D. When the underlying futures contract is trading below the strike price

81. The option writer or grantor:

    A. Has the same amount of risk as the buyer

    B. Pays no commission to his AP

    C. Always covers his sells with futures positions

    D. May be assigned a futures position

82. If December wheat is selling at a premium to March wheat of the following year and a spreader believes the spread will narrow, he would:

    A. Sell December and buy March

    B. Sell March and buy December

C. Forget it

D. None of the above

83. Trading "deep out of the money" options is a sound strategy because they are so inexpensive.

A. True

B. False

84. A customer simultaneously transferring a short from one contract month to another month in the same commodity executes a:

A. Switch

B. Straddle

C. Net trade

D. None of the above

85. A person who is long and short a commodity is a:

A. Spreader

B. Speculator

C. Hedger

D. None of the above

86. A spread can be:

A. Between different markets, same commodities

B. Within same market, different commodities

C. Between same commodities, different months

D. All of the above

87. NFA members and associate members can share commissions with customers and non-NFA members.

A. True

B. False

88. Just about anyone with enough money is suited to commodity trading.

A. True

B. False

89. If a broker asks for arbitration against an exchange member the arbitration is:

    A. Binding on both parties

    B. Mandatory for both parties

    C. Conducted by the Arbitration Committee of the exchange

    D. All of the above

90. Commissions paid by customers to brokers can be shared with other registered brokers, such as floor brokers.

    A. True

    B. False

91. If a broker holds power of attorney in an account, the broker can:

    A. Participate in a share of the profits

    B. Receive a per trade commission

    C. Trade the account

    D. All of the above

92. Stock brokers can receive trailing commissions in certain commodity trading accounts under certain circumstances.

    A. True

    B. False

93. CTAs must always provide customers with a current disclosure document.

    A. True

    B. False

94. Commission rates between a customer and a commodity broker are:

    A. The same for everyone

    B. Negotiable

    C. Set by the NFA

D. Set by the CFTC

95. If a customer lacks the proper amount of margin money to execute a trade, the broker can:

    A. Loan the customer the money

    B. Take the order anyway

    C. Wait for the customer to properly fund the account

    D. Appeal to the exchange to lower the margin requirements

96. Brokers can trade commodities for their own account as well as customer accounts.

    A. True

    B. False

97. Specifications of a commodity futures contract are established by:

    A. The exchange on which they will be traded

    B. NFA

    C. CFTC

    D. SEC

98. Customers must be sent written confirmation of trades within:

    A. 8 hours

    B. 12 hours

    C. 24 hours

    D. 36 hours

99. A customer can request money to be sent out of his trading account to the order of anyone he/she so desires.

    A. True

    B. False

Match the following:

100. _____ Commodity Broker   A. FCM

101. _____ Professional Trading Advisor   B. IB

102. _____ Firm that introduces customers   C. AP
            to clearing member of exchanges

103. _____ Sets up commodity trading pools   D. CTA

104. _____ Clearing member of futures exchanges   E. CPO

105. Floor traders can do the following in order to make sure customers get fast fills:

    A. Match two orders they have in their deck

    B. Set up trades before and after trading sessions

    C. Take off setting positions in his own account

    D. None of the above

106. Commodity brokers, known as associated persons (APs), must take a refresher course in trading each year.

    A. True

    B. False

107. Licenses granted by the NFA and CFTC are good for:

    A. 1 year

    B. 10 years

    C. As long as entity/individual is legally registered

    D. As long as entity/individual is in business

108. Customers can give their brokers cash to meet a margin call.

    A. True

    B. False

109. All customer complaints against a commodity broker must be reported to the broker's supervisor.

    A. True

    B. False

110. One of the primary tasks of APs is to put investment clubs together.

A. True

B. False

111. Commodity broker training materials are considered promotional by the NFA.

A. True

B. False

112. Copies of advertising must be kept immediately accessible for how many years after last use?

A. One year

B. Two years

C. Three years

D. Four years

E. Five years

113. The NFA considers the following as high pressure sales tactics:

A. Berating customers

B. Frequent phone calls

C. Tight deadlines for action

D. Wild promises of enormous profits

E. All of the above

114. Commodity brokers are expected to provide prospective customers with a balanced presentation concerning the risks and rewards of commodity trading.

A. True

B. False

115. Customers can open trading accounts and begin trading commodities before they complete all the account forms.

A. True

B. False

116. The NFA will conduct a compliance review of promotional material before it is used at the request of a member.

    A. True

    B. False

117. Any commodity broker can take trading discretion in a customer's account.

    A. True

    B. False

118. Professional commodity trading advisors (CTAs), who are promoting their services, must provide customers with:

    A. Disclosure document

    B. Explanation of how commodity markets work

    C. Security bond

    D. Home telephone number

119. Once properly registered with the NFA, a commodity broker can work for any firm without notifying the NFA of changes.

    A. True

    B. False

120. Commodity customers sign away all their legal rights when they execute account papers.

    A. True

    B. False

Answers to Worksheet 9

1.	D	34.	A	67.	C
2.	A	35.	A	68.	A
3.	A	36.	A	69.	C
4.	A	37.	B	70.	B
5.	D	38.	B	71.	A
6.	A	39.	B	72.	B
7.	A	40.	B	73.	B
8.	C	41.	C	74.	B
9.	D	42.	A	75.	A
10.	B	43.	B	76.	A
11.	B	44.	C	77.	A
12.	A	45.	B	78.	B
13.	A	46.	A	79.	B
14.	D	47.	B	80.	C
15.	A	48.	A	81.	D
16.	B	49.	A	82.	A
17.	D	50.	B	83.	B
18.	C	51.	B	84.	A
19.	C	52.	D	85.	A
20.	B	53.	D	86.	D
21.	B	54.	D	87.	B
22.	C	55.	B	88.	B
23.	B	56.	D	89.	D
24.	A	57.	A	90.	A
25.	A	58.	B	91.	D
26.	A	59.	A	92.	A
27.	C	60.	D	93.	B
28.	A	61.	A	94.	B
29.	B	62.	C	95.	C
30.	D	63.	C	96.	A
31.	D	64.	B	97.	A
32.	C	65.	A	98.	C
33.	A	66.	A	99.	B

100. C	107. C	114. A
101. D	108. B	115. B
102. B	109. A	116. A
103. E	110. B	117. B
104. A	111. A	118. A
105. D	112. C	119. B
106. B	113. E	120. B

Appendix 1

Glossary of Terms

Actuals—The physical or cash commodity, as distinguished from commodity futures contracts.

Administrative Law Judge (ALJ)—A CFTC official authorized to conduct a proceeding and render a decision in a formal complaint procedure.

Aggregation—The policy under which all futures positions owned or controlled by one trader or a group of traders are combined to determine reporting status and speculative limit compliance.

Arbitrage—The simultaneous purchase of one commodity against the sale of another in order to profit from distortions from usual price relationships. See also Spread, Straddle.

Arbitration—A forum for the fair and impartial settlement of disputes that the parties involved are unable to resolve between themselves. NFA's arbitration program provides a forum for resolving futures-related disputes.

Associated Person (AP)—An individual who solicits orders, customers, or customer funds on behalf of a Futures Commission Merchant, an Introducing Broker, a Commodity Trading Advisor, or a Commodity Pool Operator and who is registered with the Commodity Futures Trading Commission (CFTC) via the National Futures Association (NFA).

At the Market—See Market Order.

At the Money—An option whose strike price is equal, or approximately equal, to the current market price of the underlying futures contract.

Award—See Reparations Award.

Basis—The difference between the cash or spot price and the price of the nearby futures contract.

Bear Market (Bear/Bearish)—A market in which prices are declining. A market participant who believes prices will move lower is called a "bear." A news item is considered bearish if it is expected to produce lower prices.

Bid—An offer to buy a specific quantity of a commodity at a stated price.

Board of Trade—Any exchange or association of persons who are engaged in the business of buying or selling any commodity or receiving the same for sale on consignment. It usually means an exchange where commodity futures and/or options are traded. See also Contract Market or Exchange.

Break—A rapid and sharp price decline.

Broad Tape—The term commonly applied to newswires carrying price and background information on securities and commodities markets. This contrasts to the exchanges' own price transmission wires, which use a narrow ticker tape.

Broker—A person paid a fee or commission for acting as an agent in making contracts or sales; floor broker in commodities futures trading is person who actually executes orders on the trading floor of an exchange; account executive (associated person) is the person who deals with customers and their orders in commission house offices. See Registered Commodity Representative.

Brokerage—A fee charged by a broker for execution of a transaction—an amount charged per transaction or a percentage of the total value of the transaction; it is usually referred to as a commission fee.

Bucket, Bucketing—Illegal practice of accepting orders to buy or sell without executing such orders, and the illegal use of the customer's margin deposit without disclosing the fact of such use.

Bull Market (Bull/Bullish)—A market in which prices are rising. A participant in futures who believes prices will move higher is called a "bull." A news item is considered bullish if it is expected to bring on higher prices.

Buy or Sell on Close or Opening—To buy or sell at the end or the beginning of the trading session.

Buying Hedge (or Long Hedge)—Buying futures contracts to protect against possible increased cost of commodities slated for future uses. See Hedging.

Call (Option)—The buyer of a call option acquires the right but not the obligation to purchase a particular futures contract at a stated price on or before a particular date. Buyers of call options generally hope to profit from an increase in the futures price of the underlying commodity.

Car(s)—This is a colloquialism for futures contract(s). It came into common use when a railroad car or hopper of corn, wheat, etc., equaled the amount of a commodity in a futures contract. See Contract.

Carrying Broker—A member of a commodity exchange, usually a clearinghouse member, through whom another broker or customer chooses to clear all or some trades.

Carrying Charges—Costs incurred in warehousing the physical commodity, generally including interest, insurance, and storage.

Carryover—That part of the current supply of a commodity consisting of stocks from previous production/marketing seasons.

Cash Commodity—Actual stocks of a commodity, as distinguished from futures contracts; goods available for immediate delivery or delivery within a specified period following sale; or a commodity bought or sold with an agreement for delivery at a specified future date. See Actuals and Forward Contracting.

Cash Forward Sale—See Forward Contracting.

Certificated Stock—Stocks of a commodity that have been inspected and found to be of a quality deliverable against futures contracts, stored at the delivery points designated as regular or acceptable for delivery by the commodity exchange.

Charting—The use of graphs and charts in the technical analysis of futures markets to plot trends of price movements, average movements of price volume, and open interest. See Technical Analysis.

Churning—Excessive trading of the customer's account by a broker, who has control over the trading decisions for that account, to make more commissions while disregarding the best interests of the customer.

Clearing—The procedure through which trades are checked for accuracy. Once the trades are validated, the clearinghouse or association becomes the buyer to each seller of a futures contract and the seller to each buyer.

Clearing Member—A member of a clearinghouse or an association. All trades of a non-clearing member must be registered and eventually settled through a clearing member.

Clearinghouse—An agency connected with commodity exchanges through which all futures contracts are made, offset, or fulfilled through delivery of the actual commodity and through which financial settlement is made; often a fully chartered separate corporation rather than a division of the exchange proper.

Clearing Price—See Settlement Price.

Close (the)—The period at the end of the trading session, officially designated by the exchange, during which all transactions are considered made "at the close."

Closing Range—A range of closely related prices at which transactions took place at the closing of the market; buy and sell orders at the closing might have been filled at any point within such a range.

Commission—1) A fee charged by a broker to a customer for performance of a specific duty, such as the buying or selling of futures contracts. 2) Sometimes used to refer to the Commodity Futures Trading Commission (CFTC).

Commission Merchant—One who makes a trade, either for another member of the exchange or for a non–member client, in his or her own name and becomes liable as principal to the other party to the transaction.

Commodity—An entity of trade or commerce, services, or rights in which contracts for future delivery may be traded. Some of the contracts currently traded are wheat, corn, cotton, livestock, copper, gold, silver, oil, propane, plywood, currencies, Treasury bills, bonds, and notes.

Commodity Exchange Act—The federal act that provides for federal regulation of futures trading.

Commodity Futures Trading Commission (CFTC)—A commission set up by Congress to administer the Commodity Exchange Act which regulates trading on commodity exchanges.

Commodity Pool—An enterprise in which funds contributed by a number of persons are combined for the purpose of trading futures contracts and/or options on futures. Not the same as a joint account.

Commodity Pool Operator (CPO)—An individual or organization which operates or solicits funds for a commodity pool. Generally required to be registered with the Commodity Futures Trading Commissions.

Commodity Trading Advisor (CTA)—Individuals or firms that, for a fee, issue analysis or reports concerning commodities, advise others on the value or the advisability of trading in commodity futures, options, or leverage contracts.

Confirmation Statement—A statement sent by a commission house to a customer when a futures or options position has been initiated. The statement shows the number of contracts bought or sold and the prices at which they were bought or sold. Sometimes combined with a Purchase and Sale Statement.

Complainant—The individual who files a complaint seeking a reparations award against another individual or firm.

Consolidation—A pause in trading activity in which price moves sideways, setting the stage for the next move. Traders evaluate their positions during periods of consolidation.

Contract—A term of reference describing a unit of trading for a commodity.

Contract Grades—Standards or grades of commodities listed in the rules of the exchanges which must be met when delivering cash commodities against futures contracts. Grades are often accompanied by a schedule of discounts and premiums allowable for delivery of commodities of lesser or greater quality than the contract grade.

Contract Market—A board of trade designated by the Commodity Futures trading Commission to trade futures or option contracts on a particular commodity. Commonly used to mean any exchange on which futures are traded. See also Board of Trade and Exchange.

Contract Month—The month in which delivery is to be made in accordance with a futures contract.

Controlled Account—See Discretionary Account.

Corner—To secure control of a commodity so that its price can be manipulated.

Correction—A price reaction against the prevailing trend of the market. Common corrections often amount to 33 percent, 50 percent or 66 percent of the most recent trend movement. Sometimes referred to as a retracement.

Cost of Recovery—Administrative costs or expenses incurred in obtaining money due the complainant. Included are costs such as administrative fees, hearing room fees, charge for clerical services, travel expenses to attend the hearing, attorney's fees, and filing costs.

Cover—To offset a previous futures transaction with an equal and opposite transaction. Short covering is a purchase of futures contracts to cover an earlier sale of an equal number of contracts of the same delivery month; liquidation is the sale of futures contracts to offset the obligation to take delivery on an equal number of futures contracts of the same delivery month purchased earlier.

Current Delivery (Month)—The futures contract which will come to maturity and become deliverable during the current month; also called "spot month."

Customer Segregated Funds—See Segregated Account.

Day Order—An order that if not executed expires automatically at the end of the trading session on the day it was entered.

Day Traders—Commodity traders, generally members of the exchange active on the trading floor, who take positions in commodities, then liquidate them prior to the close of the trading day.

Dealer Option—A put or call on a physical commodity, not originating on or subject to the rules of an exchange, written by a firm which deals in the underlying cash commodity.

Debit Balance—Accounting condition where the trading losses in a customer's account exceed the amount of equity in the account.

Deck—All of the unexecuted orders in a floor broker's possession.

Default—1) In the futures market, the failure to perform on a futures contract as required by exchange rules, such as a failure to meet a margin call or to make or take delivery. 2) In reference to the Federal Farm Loan Program, the decision on the part of a producer of commodities not to repay the government loan, but instead to surrender his or her crops. This usually floods the market, driving prices lower.

Deferred Delivery—The distant delivery months in which futures trading is taking place, as distinguished from the nearby futures delivery month.

Delivery—The tender and receipt of an actual commodity or warehouse receipt or other negotiable instrument covering such commodity in settlement of a futures contract.

Deliverable Grades—See Contract Grades.

Delivery Month—A calendar month during which a futures contract matures and becomes deliverable.

Delivery Notice—Notice from the clearinghouse of a seller's intention to deliver the physical commodity against a short futures position; it precedes and is distinct from the warehouse receipt or shipping certificate, which is the instrument of transfer of ownership.

Delivery Points—Those locations designated by commodity exchanges at which stocks of a commodity represented by a futures contract may be delivered in fulfillment of the contract.

Delivery Price—The official settlement price of the trading session during which the buyer of futures contracts receives through the clearinghouse a notice of the seller's intention to deliver and the price at which the buyer must pay for the commodities represented by the futures contract.

Discount—1) A downward adjustment in price allowed for delivery of stocks of a commodity of lesser than deliverable grade against a futures contract. 2) Sometimes used to refer to the price difference between futures of different delivery months, as in the phrase "July at a discount to May," indicating that the price of the July future is lower than that of the May.

Discovery—The process which allows one party to obtain information and documents relating to the dispute from the other party(ies) in the dispute.

Discretionary Account—An arrangement by which the holder of the account gives written power of attorney to another, often a broker, to make buying and selling decisions without notification to the holder; often referred to as a managed account or controlled account.

Elasticity—A characteristic of commodities which describes the interaction of the supply, demand, and price of a commodity. A commodity is said to be elastic in demand when a price change creates an increase or decrease in consumption. The supply of a commodity is said to be elastic when a change in price creates change in the production of the commodity. Inelasticity of supply or demand exists when either is relatively unresponsive to changes in price.

Equity—The dollar value of a futures trading account if all open positions were offset at the going market price.

Exchange—An association of persons engaged in the business of buying and selling commodity futures and/or options. See also Board of Trade and Contract Market.

Exercise—Exercising an option means you elect to accept the underlying futures contract at the option's strike price.

Exercise Price—The price at which the buyer of a call (put) option may choose to exercise his right to purchase (sell) the underlying futures contract. Also called strike price.

Expiration Date—Generally the last date on which an option may be exercised.

F.O.B. (Free on Board)—Indicates that all delivery, inspection, and elevation or loading costs involved in putting commodities on board a carrier have been paid.

Feed Ratios—The variable relationships of the cost of feeding animals to market weight sales prices, expressed in ratios, such as the hog/corn ratio. These serve as indicators of the profit return or lack of it in feeding animals to market weight.

Fibonacci Number or Sequence of Numbers—The sequence of numbers (0,1,2,3,5,8,13,21,34,55,89,144,233...), discovered by the Italian mathematician Leonardo de Pise in the 13th century. It is the mathematical basis of the Elliott Wave Theory, where the first two terms of the sequence are 0 and 1 and each successive number is the sum of the previous two numbers.

Fiduciary Duty—Responsibility imposed by operation of law (from congressional policies underlying the Commodity Exchange Act) which requires that the broker act with special care in the handling of a customer's account.

First Notice Day—First day on which notices of intention to deliver cash commodities against futures contracts can be presented by sellers and received by buyers through the exchange clearinghouse.

Floor Broker—An individual who executes orders on the trading floor of an exchange for any other person.

Floor Traders—Members of an exchange who are personally present on the trading floors of exchanges to make trades for themselves and their customers. Sometimes called scalpers or locals.

Forwarding Contracting—A cash transaction common in many industries, including commodities, in which the buyer and seller agree upon delivery of a specified quality and quantity of goods at a specified future date. Specific price may be agreed upon in advance or there may be agreements that the price will be determined at the time of delivery on the basis of either the prevailing local cash price or a futures price.

Free Supply—Stocks of a commodity which are available from commercial sale, as distinguished from government-owned or controlled stocks.

Fully Disclosed—An account carried by the Futures Commission Merchant in the name of the individual customer; it is the opposite of an omnibus account.

Fundamental Analysis—An approach to analysis of futures markets and commodity futures price trends which examine the underlying factors which will affect the supply and demand of the commodity being traded in futures. (See also Technical Analysis.)

Futures Commission Merchant (FCM)—An individual or organization which solicits or accepts orders to buy or sell futures contracts or commodity options and accepts money or other assets from customers in connection with such orders. The individual or organization must be registered with the Commodity Futures Trading Commission.

Futures Contract—A standardized binding agreement to buy or sell a specified quantity or grade of a commodity at a later date, i.e., during a specified month. Futures contracts are freely transferable and can be traded only by public auction on designated exchanges.

Futures Industry Association (FIA)—The national trade association for the futures industry.

Gap—A trading day during which the daily price range is completely above or below the previous day's range causing a gap between them. Some traders then look for a retracement to "fill the gap."

Grantor—A person who sells an option and assumes the obligation but not the right to sell (in the case of a call) or buy (in the case of a put) the underlying futures contract or commodity at the exercise price. See also Writer.

Gross Processing Margin (GPM)—Refers to the difference between the cost of soybeans and the combined sales income of the soybean oil and meal which results from processing soybeans.

Guided Account—An account that is part of a program directed by a Commodity Trading Advisor (CTA) or Futures Commission Merchant (FCM). The CTA or FCM plans the trading strategies. The customer is advised to enter and/or liquidate specific trading positions. However, approval to enter the order must be given by the customer. These programs usually require a minimum initial investment and may include a trading strategy that will use only a part of the investment at any given time.

Hedging—The sale of futures contracts in anticipation of future sales of cash commodities as a protection against possible price declines or the purchase of futures contracts in anticipation of future purchases of cash commodities as a protection against increasing costs. See also Buying Hedge, Selling Hedge.

Inelasticity—A characteristic that describes the interdependence of the supply, demand, and price of a commodity. A commodity is inelastic when a price change does not create an increase or decrease in consumption; inelasticity exists when supply and demand are relatively unresponsive to changes in price. See also Elasticity.

Initial Margin—Customers' funds required at the time a futures position is established, or an option is sold, to assure performance of the customer's obligations. Margin in commodities is not a down payment, as it is in securities. See also Margin.

In the Money—An option having intrinsic value. A call is in the money if its strike price is below the current price of the underlying futures contract. A put is in the money if its strike price is above the current price of the underlying futures contract.

Intrinsic Value—The absolute value of the "in the money" amount; that is, the amount that would be realized if an in the money option were exercised.

Introducing Broker (IB)—A firm or individual that solicits and accepts commodity futures orders from customers but does not accept money, securities, or property from the customer. An IB must be registered with the Commodity Futures Trading Commission and must carry all of its accounts through an FCM on a fully disclosed basis.

Inverted Market—Futures market in which the nearer months are selling at premiums over the more distant months; it is, characteristically, a market in which supplies are currently in shortage.

Invisible Supply—Uncounted stocks of a commodity in the hands of wholesalers, manufacturers, and producers which cannot be identified accurately; the stocks are outside commercial channels but theoretically available to the market.

Last Trading Day—Day on which trading ceases for the maturing (current) delivery month.

Leverage—Essentially, it allows an investor to establish a position in the marketplace by depositing funds that are less than the value of the contract.

Leverage Contract—A standardized agreement calling for the delivery of a commodity with payments against the total cost spread out over a period of time. Its principal characteristics include standard units and quality of a commodity and of terms and conditions of the contract, payment and maintenance of margin close out by offset or delivery (after payment in full) and no right to or interest in a specific lot of the commodity. Leverage contracts are not traded on exchanges.

Leverage Transaction Merchant (LTM)—The firm or individual through whom leverage contracts are entered. LTMs must be registered with the Commodity Futures Trading Commission.

Life of Contract—Period between the beginning of trading in a particular future and the expiration of trading in the delivery month.

Limit—See position limit, price limit, variable limit, and reporting limit.

Limit Move—A price that has advanced or declined the limit permitted during one trading session as fixed by the rules of a contract market.

Limit Order—An order in which the customer sets a limit on either price or time of execution, or both, as contrasted with a market order, which implies that the order should be filled at the most favorable price as soon as possible.

Liquidation—Usually the sale of futures contracts to offset the obligation to take delivery of an equal number of futures contracts of the same delivery month purchased earlier. Sometimes refers to the purchase of futures contracts to offset a previous sale.

Liquidity (or Liquid Market)—A broadly traded market where buying and selling can be accomplished with small price changes and bid and offer price spreads are narrow.

Liquid Market—A market where selling and buying can be accomplished easily due to the presence of many interested buyers and sellers.

Loan Program—The primary means of government agricultural price support operations. The government lends money to farmers at announced rates, with using the crops as collateral. Default on these loans is the primary method by which the government acquires stocks of agricultural commodities.

Long—One who has bought a cash commodity or a commodity futures contract, in contrast to a short, who has sold a cash commodity or futures contract.

Long Hedge—Buying futures contracts to protect against possible increased prices of commodities. See also Hedging.

Maintenance Margin—The amount of money that must be maintained on deposit while a futures position is open. If the equity in a customer's account drops under the maintenance margin level, the broker must issue a call for money that will restore the customer's equity in the account to required initial levels. See also Margin.

Margin—In the futures industry, it is an amount of money deposited by both buyers and sellers of futures contracts to ensure performance against the contract. It is not a down payment.

Margin Call—A call from a brokerage firm to a customer to bring margin deposits back up to minimum levels required by exchange regulations; similarly, a request by the clearing house to a clearing member firm to make additional deposits to bring clearing margins back to minimum levels required by clearinghouse rules.

Market Order—An order to buy or sell futures contracts which is to be filled at the best possible price and as soon as possible. A limit order, in contrast, may specify requirements for price or time of execution. See also Limit Order.

Maturity—Period within which a futures contract can be settled by delivery of the actual commodity; the period between the first notice day and the last trading day of a commodity futures contract.

Maximum Price Fluctuation—See Limit Move.

Minimum Price Fluctuation—See Point.

Misrepresentation—An untrue or misleading statement concerning a material fact relied upon by a customer when making his/her decision about an investment.

Momentum Indicator—A line that is plotted to represent the difference between today's price and the price of a fixed number of days ago. Momentum can be measured as the difference between today's price and the current value of a moving average. Often referred to as momentum oscillators.

Moving Average—A mathematical procedure to smooth or eliminate the fluctuations in data. Moving averages emphasize the direction of a trend, confirm trend reversals, and smooth out price and volume fluctuations or "noise" that can confuse interpretation of the market.

National Association of Futures Trading Advisors (NAFTA)—The national trade association of Commodity Pool Operators (CPOs, Commodity Trading Advisors (CTAs)), and related industry participants.

National Futures Association (NFA)—The industry-wide self-regulatory organization of the futures industry.

Nearby Delivery (Month)—The futures contract closest to maturity.

Nearbys—The nearest delivery months of a futures market.

New Asset Value—The value of each unit of a commodity pool. Basically, it is a calculation of assets minus liabilities plus or minus the value of open positions (marked-to-the-market) divided by the number of units.

Net Performance—An increase or decrease in net asset value exclusive of additions, withdrawals, and redemptions.

Net Position—The difference between the open long (buy) contracts and the open short (sell) contracts held by any one person in any one futures contract month, or in all months combined.

Nominal Price—Declared price for a futures month sometimes used in place of a closing price when no recent trading has taken place in that particular delivery month; usually it is an average of the bid and asked prices.

Nondisclosure—Failure to disclose a material fact needed by the customer to make a decision regarding an investment.

Normalizing—An adjustment to data, such as a price series, to put it within normal or more standard range. A technique used to develop a trading system.

Notice Day—See First Notice Day.

Notice of Delivery—See Delivery Notice.

Offer—An indication of willingness to sell at a given price—the opposite of bid.

Offset—The liquidation of a purchase of futures through the sale of an equal number of contracts of the same delivery months or the covering of a short sale of futures contracts through the purchase of an equal number of contracts of the same delivery month. Either action transfers the obligation to make or take delivery of the actual commodity to someone else.

Omnibus Account—An account carried by one futures commission merchant with another where the transactions of two or more persons are combined, rather than designated separately, and the identity of the individual accounts is not disclosed.

Open—The period at the beginning of the trading session officially designated by the exchange during which all transactions are considered made "at the open."

Open Interest—The total number of futures contracts of a given commodity which have not yet been offset by opposite futures transactions nor fulfilled by delivery of the actual commodity; the total number of open transactions where each transaction has a buyer and a seller.

Open Outcry—Method of public auction for making bids and offers in the trading pits or rings of commodity exchanges.

Opening Range—The range of closely related prices at which transactions took place at the opening of the market; buying and selling orders at the opening which might be filled at any point within such a range.

Open Trade Equity—The unrealized gain or loss on open positions.

Option Contract—A unilateral contract which gives the buyer the right, but not the obligation, to buy or sell a specified quantity of a commodity or a futures contract at a specific price within a specified period of time, regardless of the market price of that commodity or futures contract. The seller of the option has the obligation to sell the commodity or futures contract or buy it from the option buyer at the exercise price if the option is exercised. See also Call (Option) and Put (Option).

Option Premium—The money, securities, or property the buyer pays to the writer(grantor) for granting an option contract.

Option Seller—See Grantor.

Order Execution—The handling of a customer order by a broker, including receiving the order verbally or in writing from the customer, transmitting it to the trading floor of the exchange where the transaction takes place, and returning confirmation (fill price) of the completed order to the customer.

Orders—See Market Order, Stop Order.

Original Margin—The term applied to the initial deposit of margin money required of clearing member firms by clearinghouse rules; it parallels the initial margin deposit required of customers.

Out of the Money—A call option with a strike price higher or a put option with a strike price lower than the current market value of the underlying asset.

Overbought—A technical opinion that the market price has risen too steeply and too fast in relation to underlying fundamental factors.

Oversold—A technical opinion that the market price has declined too steeply and too fast in relation to underlying fundamental factors.

P & S Statement—See Purchase and Sale Statement.

Par—A particular price, 100 percent of principal value.

Parity—A theoretically equal relationship between farm product prices and all other prices. In farm program legislation, parity is defined in such a manner that the purchasing power of a unit of an agricultural commodity is maintained at its level during an earlier historical base period.

Pit—A specially constructed arena on the trading floor of some exchanges where trading in a futures or options contract is conducted by open outcry. On other exchanges, the term "ring" designates the trading area for a futures or options contract.

Point—The minimum fluctuation in futures prices or options premiums.

Point Balance—A statement prepared by Futures Commission Merchants to show profit or loss on all open contracts by computing them to an official closing or settlement price.

Pool—See Commodity Pool.

Position—A market commitment. For example, a buyer of futures contracts is said to have a long position and, conversely, a seller of futures contracts is said to have a short position.

Position Limit—The maximum number of futures contracts that one can hold in certain regulated commodities, according to the provisions of the CFTC. Reference Reporting Limits.

Position Trader—A commodity trader who either buys or sells contracts and holds them for an extended period of time, as distinguished from a day trader, who will normally initiate and liquidate a futures position within a single trading session.

Premium—1) The additional payment allowed by exchange regulations for delivery of higher-than-required standards or grades of a commodity against a futures contract. In speaking of price relationships between different delivery months of a given commodity, one is said to be trading at a premium over another when its price is greater than that of the other. 2) It can also mean the amount paid a grantor or writer of an option by a trader.

Price Limit—Maximum price advance or decline from the previous day settlement price permitted for a commodity in one trading session by the rules of the exchange.

Primary Markets—The principal market for the purchase and sale of a cash commodity.

Principal—Refers to a person who is a principal of a particular entity; 1) Any person including, but not limited to, a sole proprietor, general partner, officer or director, or person occupying a similar status or performing similar functions, having the power, directly or indirectly, through agreement or otherwise, to exercise a controlling influence over the activities of the entity; 2) Any holder or any beneficial owner of 10 percent or more of the outstanding shares of any class of stock of the entity; 3) Any person who has contributed 10 percent or more of the capital of the entity.

Private Wires—Wires leased by various firms and news agencies for the transmission of information to branch offices and subscriber clients.

Proceeding Clerk—The member of the commission's staff in the Office of Proceedings who maintains the Commission's reparations docket, assigns reparation cases to an appropriate CFTC official, and acts as custodian of the records of proceedings.

Producer—A person or entity that produces (grows, mines, etc.) a commodity.

Public Elevators—Grain storage facilities, licensed and regulated by state and federal agencies, in which space is rented out to whomever is willing to pay for it; some are also approved by the commodity exchanges for delivery of commodities against futures contracts.

Purchase Price—The total actual cost paid by a person for entering into a commodity option transaction, including premium, commission, or any other direct or indirect charges.

Purchase and Sale Statement (P&S)—A statement sent by a commission house to a customer when a futures or options position has been liquidated or offset. The statement shows the number of contracts bought or sold, the gross profit or loss, the commission charges, and the net profit or loss on the transaction. Sometimes combined with a confirmation statement.

Put (Option)—An option that gives the option buyer the right, but not the obligation, to sell the underlying futures contract at a particular price on or before a particular date.

Pyramiding—The use of profits on existing futures positions as margins to increase the size of the position, normally in successively smaller increments, such as the use of profits on the purchase of five futures contracts as margin to purchase an additional four contracts, whose profits will in turn be used to margin an additional three contracts.

Quotation—The actual price or the bid or ask price of either cash commodities or futures or options contracts at a particular time. Often called Quote.

Rally—An upward movement of prices. See also Recovery.

Rally Top—The point where a rally stalls. A bull move will usually make several rally tops over its life.

Rang—The difference between the high and low price of a commodity during a given period, usually a single trading session.

Reaction—A short term countertrend movement of prices.

Recovery—An upward movement of prices following a decline.

Receivership—A situation in which a receiver has been appointed. A receiver is a person appointed by a court to take custody and to control, and to manage the property or funds of another, pending judicial action concerning them.

Registered Commodity Representative (RCR)—See Broker or Associated Person (AP).

Regulations (CFTC)—The regulations adopted and enforced by the federal overseer of futures markets, the Commodity Futures Trading Commission, in order to administer the Commodity Exchange Act.

Reparations—Compensation payable to a wronged party in a futures or options transaction. The term is used in conjunction with the Commodity Futures Trading Commission's customer claims procedure to recover civil damages.

Reparations Award—The amount of monetary damages a respondent may be ordered to pay to a complainant.

Reporting Limit—Sizes of positions set by the exchange and/or by the CFTC at or above which commodity traders must make daily reports to the exchange and/or the CFTC as to the size of the position by commodity, by delivery month, and according to the purpose of trading, i.e., speculative or hedging.

Resistance—The price level where a trend stalls. It is the opposite of a support level. Prices must build momentum to move through resistance.

Respondents—The individuals or firms against which the complaint is filed and a reparations award is sought.

Retender—The right of holders of futures contracts who have been tendered a delivery notice through the clearinghouse to offer the notice for sale on the open market, liquidating their obligation to take delivery under the contract; it is applicable only to certain commodities and only within a specified period of time.

Retracement—A price movement in the opposite direction of the prevailing trend. See Correction.

Ring—A circular area on the trading floor of an exchange where traders and brokers stand while executing futures or options trades. Some exchanges use pits rather than rings.

Round Lot—A quantity of a commodity equal in size to the corresponding futures contract for the commodity, as distinguished from a job lot, which may be larger or smaller than the contract.

Round Turn—The combination of an initiating purchase or sale of a futures contract and offsetting sale or purchase of an equal number of futures contracts to the same delivery month. Commission fees for commodity transactions cover the round turn.

Rules (NFA)—The standards and requirements to which participants who are required to be Members of National Futures Association must subscribe and conform.

Sample Grade—In commodities, usually the lowest quality acceptable for delivery in satisfaction of futures contracts. See Contract Grades.

Scalper—A speculator on the trading floor of an exchange who buys and sells rapidly, with small profits or losses, holding positions for only a short time during a trading session. Typically, a scalper will stand ready to buy at a fraction below the last transaction price and to sell at a fraction above, thus creating market liquidity.

Security Deposit—See Margin.

Segregated Account—A special account used to hold and separate customer's assets from those of the broker or firm.

Selling Hedge—Selling futures contracts to protect against possible decreased prices of commodities which will be sold in the future. See Hedging and/or Short Hedge.

Settlement Price—The closing price, or a price within the range of closing prices, which is used as the official price in determining net gains or losses at the close of each trading session.

Short—One who has sold a cash commodity or a commodity futures contract; a long, in contrast, is one who has bought a cash commodity or futures contract.

Short Hedge—Selling futures to protect against possible decreasing prices of commodities. See also Hedging.

Speculator—One who attempts to anticipate commodity price changes and make profits through the sale and/or purchase of commodity futures contracts. A speculator with a forecast of advancing prices hopes to profit by buying futures contracts, then liquidating the obligation to take delivery with a later sale of an equal number of futures of the same delivery month at a higher price. A speculator with a forecast of declining prices hopes to profit by selling commodity futures contracts, then covering the obligation to deliver with a later purchase of futures at a lower price.

Spot—Market for the immediate delivery of the product and immediate payment. May also refer to the nearest delivery month of a futures contract.

Spot Commodity—See Cash Commodity.

Spread (or Straddle)—The purchase of one futures delivery month against the sale of another futures delivery month of the same commodity; the purchase of one delivery month of one commodity against the sale of the same delivery month of a different commodity; or the purchase of one commodity in one market against the sale of that commodity in another market, to take advantage of and profit from the distortions from the normal price relationships that sometimes occur. The term is also used to refer to the difference between the price of one futures month and the price of another month of the same commodity. See also Arbitrage.

Stop Loss—A risk management technique used to close out a losing position at a given point. See Stop Order.

Stop Order—An order that becomes a market order when a particular price level is reached. A sell stop is placed below the market, a buy stop is placed above the market. Sometimes referred to as a Stop Loss Order.

Strike Price—See Exercise Price.

Support—A price level at which a declining market has stopped falling. It is the opposite of a resistance price range. Once this level is reached, the market trades sideways for a period of time.

Switch—Liquidation of a position in one delivery month of a commodity and simultaneous initiation of a similar position in another delivery month of the same commodity. When used by hedgers, this tactic is referred to as "rolling forward" the hedge.

Technical Analysis—An approach to analysis of futures markets and anticipated future trends of commodity prices. It examines the technical factors of market activity. Technicians normally examine patterns of price range, rates of change, changes in volume of trading, and open interest. There data are often charted to show trends and formations which serve as indicators of likely future price movements.

Tender—The act on the part of the seller of futures contracts of giving notice to the clearinghouse, that he or she intends to deliver the physical commodity in satisfaction of the futures contract. The clearinghouse in turn, passes along the notice to the oldest buyer of record in that delivery month of the commodity. See also Retender.

Tick—Refers to a change in price, up or down. See also Point.

Ticker Tape—A continuous paper tape transmission of commodity or security prices, volume, and other trading and market information which operates on private or lease wires by the exchanges. It is available to their member firms and other interested parties on a subscription basis.

Time Value—Any amount by which an option premium exceeds the option's intrinsic value.

To-Arrive Contract—A type of deferred shipment in which the price is based on delivery at the destination point. The seller pays the freight in shipping it to that point.

Traders—1) People who trade for their own account. 2) Employees of dealers or institutions who trade for their employer's account.

Trading Range—An established set of price boundaries with a high and a low price within which a market will spend a marked period of time.

Transferable Notice—See Retender.

Trend Line—A line drawn that connects either a series of highs or lows in a trend. The trend line can represent either support (as in an uptrend line) or resistance (as in a downtrend line). Consolidations are marked by horizontal trend lines.

Unauthorized Trading—Purchase or sale of commodity futures or options for a customer's account without the customer's permission.

Underlying Futures Contract—The specific futures contract that the option conveys the right to buy (in the case of a call) or sell (in the case of a put).

Variable Limit—A price system that allows price movements for larger than normally allowed price movements under certain conditions. In periods of extreme volatility, some exchanges permit trading and price levels to exceed regular daily limits. At such times, margins may be automatically increased.

Variation Margin Call—A mid-session call by the clearinghouse on a clearing member requiring the deposit of additional funds to bring clearing margin monies up to minimum levels in relation to changing prices and the clearing member's net position.

Volatility—A measure of a commodity's tendency to move up and down in price based on its daily price history over a period of time.

Volume of Trade—The number of contracts traded during a specified period of time.

Warehouse Receipt—Document guaranteeing the existence and availability of a given quantity and quality of a commodity in storage; it is commonly used as the instrument of transfer of ownership in both cash and futures transactions.

Wirehouse—See Futures Commission Merchant (FCM).

Write—See Grantor.

Note—This glossary is included to assist the reader. It is not a set of legal definitions, nor a guide to interpreting the Commodity Exchange Act or any other legal instrument. For all legal assistance, contact your personal attorney.

Appendix 2

Sources for More Information

We'd first like to call your attention to two reference guides that will provide you with a broad overview of information you can access. Then we'll zero in on several books we believe are particularly valuable for future study.

For Publications—*The Individual Investor's Guide to Investment Publications* describes more than 150 newsletters, magazines and other publications plus software and financial databases. The futures section fills sixteen pages. Here's a sample of our listing to give you an idea of the information provided.

Futures and Options Factors—The Futures Portfolio Advisor (188)

　　　Publisher—Wasendorf & Associates, Inc.; 802 Main Street., P.O. Box 849, Cedar Falls, IA 50613, 319/268-0441

　　　Editor/Background: Russell R. Wasendorf

Sixteen years experience in the futures market, author of *Commodities Trading: The Essential Primer* (Dow Jones/Irwin 1984), founder of Center for Futures Education.

Philosophy—To provide long-term investment strategies in the futures and options markets using portfolio theory and index analysis.

Description—Publishes a unique series of index charts each week. These charts are the result of extensive research into Index Analysis, an adaptation of the Dow Theory. Called the Wasendorf Series of Commodity Indexes, these charts are analyzed in the newsletter and specific recommendations for trades in individual futures markets are advised. Covers all futures markets including grains, meats, metals, food/fiber, stock indexes, currencies, debt instruments, and petroleum markets. A daily telephone hotline is included.

Format—Newsletter; Frequency—Weekly; No. Pages—8; First Issue—12/80; Circulation—2,000; Subscription Prices—one year, $228

Previously Known As—The Futures Portfolio Advisor

More information about this guide can be obtained from International Publishing Corporation, Inc., 625 N. Michigan Ave., Suite 1920, Chicago, IL 60611. Phone: 312/943-7354. If you'd like a sample of our newsletter, just give Wasendorf & Associates a call at 1-800-553-1711.

For Other Services—Brokerage firms, commodity trading advisors (CTAs), commodity pool operators (CPOs), computer/electronic price quotation and news services, publishers, professional services (education, legal), exchanges, futures and option industry organizations and more, you can browse through the *Futures Magazine's Annual Reference Guide* published each June. This annual reference guide covers a very wide range of products and services, but provides only the name, address, phone number and product-service category for most firms. It will give you a list of firms to contact. It is available from Oster Communication, 219 Parkade, Cedar Falls, IA 50613. Phone: 319/277-6341.

For Reference Books—Naturally, you should contact your local library. There are many very good ones. We'd like to single out the following as being particularly useful.

Baratz, Morton, *The Investor's Guide to Futures Money Management*, Revised Edition, (1989) LJR Communications, Inc., Columbia, MD.

Bernstein, Jake, *Facts on Futures: Insights and Strategies for Winning in the Futures Markets*, (1987) Probus Publishing Company, Chicago, IL.

Bernstein, Jake, *The Investor's Quotient*, (1981) John Wiley & Sons, New York, NY.

Chance, Don M., *An Introduction to Options and Futures*, (1989) The Dryden Press, Chicago, IL.

Chicago Board of Trade Commodity Trading Manual, (1989) Board of Trade of the City of Chicago (updated and revised approximately every other year. Check for latest edition).

Dewey, Edward R., *Cycles, Selected Writings*, (1970) Foundation for the Study of Cycles, Pittsburgh, PA.

Dunn, D. and Hargitt, E., *Point and Figure Commodity Trading: A Computer Evaluation*, (1971) Dunn and Hargitt, West Lafayette, IN.

Elliott, R.N., *The Wave Principle*, (1938) Elliott, New York, NY.

Gann, William D., *How to Make Profits in Commodities*, (1951) Lambert-Gann, Pomeroy, WA.

Herbst, Anthony F., *Commodity Futures: Markets, Methods of Analysis, and Management of Risks*, (1986) John Wiley & Sons Inc., New York, NY.

Hieronymus, Thomas, *Economics of Futures Trading for Commercial and Personal Profit*, (1977) Commodity Research Bureau, New York, NY.

Jiler, William L., *How Charts Can Help You in the Stock Market*, (1962) Standard & Poor's Corporation, New York, NY.

Kaufman, Perry J., *Handbook of Futures Markets: Commodity, Financial, Stock Index, and Options*, (1984) John Wiley & Sons, Inc., New York, NY.

Kolb, Robert W., *Understanding Futures Markets*, 3rd Edition, (1991) Kolb Publishing Inc., Miami, FL.

Labuszewski, John and Singuefield, Jeanne Cavins, *Inside the Commodity Options Market*, (1985) John Wiley & Sons, New York, NY.

Luft, Carl F., *The Investor's Self-Teaching Seminar Series: Understanding and Trading Futures*, (1991) Probus Publishing Company, Chicago, IL.

Natenberg, Sheldon, *Option Volatility and Pricing Strategies*, (1988) Probus Publishing Company, Chicago, IL.

Petzel, Todd E., *Financial Futures and Options*, (1989) Quorum Books, New York, NY.

Schwager, Jack O., *A Complete Guide to the Futures Markets: Fundamental Analysis, Technical Analysis, Trading, Spreads, and Options*, (1984) John Wiley & Sons Inc., New York, NY.

Shaleen, Kenneth H., *Volume and Open Interest*, (1991) Probus Publishing Company, Chicago, IL.

Siegel, Daniel R. and Siegel, Diane F., *The Futures Markets*, (1990) Probus Publishing Company, Chicago, IL.

Sklarew, Arthur, *Techniques of a Professional Commodity Chart Analyst*, (1980) Commodity Research Bureau, Inc., New York, NY.

Teweles, Richard J., Harlow, Charles V. and Stone, Herbert L., *The Commodity Futures Game: Who Wins? Who Loses? Why? (1974) McGraw-Hill, New York, NY.*

Wasendorf, Russell R., *Commodities Trading: The Essential Primer*, (1985) Dow Jones-Irwin, Homewood, IL.

For Compliance Assistance, the following organizations regulate the futures and securities industries or they have related enforcement powers.

Alliance Against Fraud Telemarketing
c/o National Consumers League
815 15th St. NW, Suite 516
Washington, DC 20005

American Association of Individual Investors
612 North Michigan Avenue
Chicago, IL 60611
312/280-0170

Commodity Futures Trading Commission
2033 K Street NW
Washington, DC 20581
202/254-6387

Council of Better Business Bureaus
1515 Wilson Boulevard
Arlington, VA 22209
703/276-0100

Federal Bureau of Investigation
Justice Department
9th St. & Pennsylvania Ave., NW
Washington, DC 20580
202/326-3650

Federal Trade Commission
6th St. & Pennsylvania Ave., NW
Washington, DC 20580
202/326-3650

National Association of Securities Dealers
1735 K Street, NW
Washington, DC 20006
202/728-8044

National Consumers League
815 15th St., NW
Suite 516
202/639-8140

National Futures Association
200 W. Madison, Suite 1600
Chicago, IL 60606
Toll-free: 800/621-3570
In IL: 800/572-9400

North American Securities Administration Association
2930 SW Wanamaker Drive
Suite 5
Topeka, KS 66614
913/273-2600

Securities and Exchange Commission
450 Fifth St., NW
Washington, DC 20006
202/728-8233

United States Postal Service
Chief Postal Inspector
Room 3021
Washington, DC 20260-2100
202/268-4267

Here's a list of the exchanges. Each has a public information department and will send information on request.

AMEX Commodities Corp.
86 Trinity Place
New York, New York 10006
212/306-8940

Board of Trade of Kansas City, Missouri, Inc.
4800 Main Street
Kansas City, Missouri 64112
816/753-7500

Chicago Board of Trade
141 West Jackson Boulevard
Chicago, Illinois 60604
312/435-3620

Chicago Mercantile Exchange
30 S. Wacker Drive
Chicago, Illinois 60606
312/930-1000

Chicago Rice & Cotton Exchange
444 West Jackson Boulevard
Chicago, Illinois 60606
312/341-3078

Coffee, Sugar & Cocoa Exchange
4 World Trade Center
New York, New York 10048
212/938-2800

Commodity Exchange Incorporated (COMEX)
4 World Trade Center
New York, New York 10048
212/938-2900

MidAmerica Commodity Exchange
141 West Jackson Boulevard
Chicago, Illinois 60604
312/341-3000

Minneapolis Grain Exchange
150 Grain Exchange Building
Minneapolis, Minnesota 55415
612/338-6212

New York Cotton Exchange
4 World Trade Center
New York, New York 10048
212/938-2702

New York Futures Exchange
20 Broad Street
New York, New York 10005
212/656-4949

New York Mercantile Exchange
4 World Trade Center
New York, New York 10048
212/938-2222

Philadelphia Board of Trade
Philadelphia Stock Exchange Building
1900 Market Street
Philadelphia, Pennsylvania 19105
215/496-5000

Index

X
"Xs" and "O" (point & figure charts), 47

Y
Your Inner Path to Investment Success,
106-08

Z
Zero based investment, 136

About the Authors

Russell R. Wasendorf manages his own introducing brokerage firm, Wasendorf & Son Company. Previously, he directed the Commodity Education Institute, which trained hundreds of futures brokers and traders. By the early 1980s, Mr. Wasendorf had developed his proprietary indexes and began the development of his index analysis system. By the mid-1980s, he had written *Commodities Trading: The Essential Primer* (Dow Jones-Irwin, 1985), began a newsletter to track his trading system, "Futures and Options Factors," and launched a commodity price charting service "Pocket Charts."

Thomas A. McCafferty's involvement in the cash commodities and futures industries goes back to 1973. He has traded futures for his own account and supervised brokers who traded for others. Additionally, he has a strong background in sales and marketing and is the author of *In-House Telemarketing: A Master Plan for Starting and Managing a Profitable Telemarketing Program* (Probus, 1987). Currently, Mr. McCafferty oversees the branch office system for Wasendorf & Son Company, an introducing broker.

Mr. Wasendorf and Mr. McCafferty authored *All About Futures* (Probus, 1992).

Dear Reader:

We hope you enjoyed this book. More importantly, we hope it answered your questions regarding investing in the commodities market. As you've learned, not everyone is suited to it. The risks involved are considerable—matched only by the potential returns.

If you'd like to follow some of these markets for awhile, we'll be happy to send you four free issues of our commodity price chart service, "Pocket Charts." It contains forty-eight individual charts covering thirty-eight distinct futures markets. Here's a breakdown:

◆ 5 METALS—Palladium, Platinum, Gold, Copper and Silver

◆ 14 FINANCIALS—British Pound, Dollar Index, D-Mark, Canadian Dollar, Japanese Yen, Swiss Franc, S & P 500, NYSE Comp. Index, Muni Bond, Value Line, T-Notes, T-Bonds, T-Bills, Eurodollars.

◆ 6 GRAINS (12 Charts)—Corn (2 delivery months), Oats, Soybeans (2 delivery months), Soybean Oil, Soybean Meal, Chicago CBT Wheat (2 delivery months), Kansas City Wheat, Minneapolis Wheat.

◆ 4 MEATS—Live Cattle, Feeder Cattle, Live Hogs, and Pork Bellies.

◆ 6 FOOD & FIBERS—Cocoa, World Sugar, Orange Juice, Coffee, Lumber, Cotton.

◆ 3 PETROLEUMS—Heating Oil, Crude Oil, Unleaded Gas.

◆ 5 WASENDORF INDEXES—Composite, Grain, Meat, Metal, Food/Fiber.

To receive your free issues, simply mail the coupon on the next page or give us a call at 1-800-553-1711.

Last of all, we'd like to thank you for the time, effort, and money you've invested in the book. We sincerely wish you the best of luck with all your investments.

Sincerely,
Thomas McCafferty and Russell R. Wasendorf
Authors of *All About Commodities*

Yes ... I'd like to follow the markets for awhile. Please send me four (4) weeks of your commodity price charting service, "Pocket Charts" at no cost or obligation.

Call **1/800-553-1711**

Or mail coupon to:

Wasendorf & Associates, Inc.
802 Main Street, P.O. Box 849
Cedar Falls, IA 50613

Name_____

Address _____

City _____

State _____

Zip_____

Phone (_____) _____

About the Publisher

PROBUS PUBLISHING COMPANY

Probus Publishing Company fills the informational needs of today's business professional by publishing authoritative, quality books on timely and relevant topics, including:

- Investing
- Futures/Options Trading
- Banking
- Finance
- Marketing and Sales
- Manufacturing and Project Management
- Personal Finance, Real Estate, Insurance and Estate Planning
- Entrepreneurship
- Management

Probus books are available at quantity discounts when purchased for business, educational or sales promotional use. For more information, please call the Director, Corporate/Institutional Sales at 1-800-PROBUS-1, or write:

Director, Corporate/Institutional Sales
Probus Publishing Company
1925 N. Clybourn Avenue
Chicago, Illinois 60614
FAX (312) 868-6250